AWAKEN YOUR

GOOD VIBE GANGSTA

SIMPLE STEPS FOR PERSONAL GROWTH, SOCIAL IMPACT, AND LEADERSHIP.

*Written in
English & Spanish
by*

Jimmy & Joey
FLORES

"The Flores Brothers"

Staten House
New York, New York
2024

The Flores Brothers

Copyright © 2024 by GVG Lifestyle, LLC

Published by Staten House | New York, New York

Staten House

First Edition, 2024

ISBN: 979-8-89496-026-5 (paperback)

ISBN: 979-8-89496-029-6 (e-book)

ISBN: 979-8-89496-022-7 (audio)

Library of Congress Control Number: 2024913266

All rights reserved. No part of this publication may be reproduced, stored in a retrieval system, or transmitted in any form or by any means, electronic, mechanical, photocopying, recording, scanning, or otherwise, without the prior written permission in writing from the publisher or authors.

This publication is designed to provide accurate and authoritative information regarding the subject matter covered. It is sold with the understanding that neither the authors nor the publisher is engaged in rendering legal, investment, accounting, or other professional services. While the authors have used their best efforts in preparing this book, they make no representations or warranties with respect to the accuracy or completeness of the contents of this book and specifically disclaim any implied warranties of merchantability or fitness for a particular purpose. No warranty may be created or extended by sales representatives or written sales materials. The advice and strategies contained herein may not be suitable for your situation. You should consult with a professional when appropriate. The authors shall not be liable for any loss of profit or any other commercial damages, including but not limited to special, incidental, consequential, personal, or other damages.

To our incredible reader:

You know how it goes. You pick up a book, flip to the dedication, and find that, once again, the authors have dedicated a book to someone else and not you.

Not this time.

This one is for you and our late father, Mario Alejandro Flores Sarti.

You may not be able to change the entire world, but you can definitely change the world around you.

— MARÍA SARTI

TABLE OF CONTENTS

FOREWORD 6
INTRODUCTION 10
CHAPTER 1 18
   Maintain Youthful Energy 18
CHAPTER 2 52
   Pursue Passions 52
CHAPTER 3 81
   Accept Failure 81
CHAPTER 4 115
   Afford To Care 115
CHAPTER 5 149
   Leave Unique Fingerprints 149
CHAPTER 6 189
   Make Splendid Mistakes 189
CHAPTER 7 216
   Enjoy The Ride 216
CONCLUSION 252
END NOTES 258
AFTERWORD 259
ABOUT THE AUTHORS 262
ACKNOWLEDGMENTS 270

FOREWORD

Awaken Your Good Vibe Gangsta

Dear Reader,

As a lifelong supporter of positive change and the devoted mother of Jimmy and Joey, I am excited to introduce you to a transformative book that not only integrates the values the authors cherish but also offers a powerful blueprint for personal and societal evolution. *Awaken Your Good Vibe Gangsta* is more than a book inspired by the authors' historic commencement speech; it is a sweeping call to action, inspiring you to radically rethink how you perceive and interact with the world.

The pain of unfulfilled potential and disconnected lives is deep and often silent, further magnified by an epidemic of loneliness and isolation. Many walk through life unaware of the personal, financial, and social costs of not addressing this void. This book diagnoses the pain of feeling disconnected from one's true potential and community and lays out the significant costs of continuing on that path.

Each chapter in this book sheds new light on this problem, offering not only a diagnosis but also a hopeful prognosis. This book provides an actionable roadmap, guiding you toward a life rich with purpose and positive impact. The journey from passive existence to active engagement is mapped out with clear, actionable steps, ensuring you have all the tools you need to transform your life and the lives of those around you.

The value of this book far exceeds its cost, delivering insights and strategies that can revolutionize not only how you see yourself but also how you influence the world. It offers you a return on your investment that is not just substantial but transformative, creating more than one hundred times the value for you compared to its cost. Moreover, the value it offers you surpasses what it provides to the authors. Their primary aim is not profit but to enrich humanity's body of knowledge and to inspire real, lasting change.

From the first page to the last, this book is packed with invaluable insights. Each chapter builds on the previous one, culminating in a complete guide that is invaluable in its entirety. The payoff of engaging deeply with this book is immense, equipping you to achieve personal success and use that success as a catalyst for broader societal betterment.

As you dive into this book, remember that it is a call to action. It is an invitation to awaken the potent forces of positivity and capability within you. Let this book be your guide as you take each step toward becoming not just a leader, but a visionary who actively crafts a better world through every thought, interaction, and decision.

When you decide to acquire *Awaken Your Good Vibe Gangsta*, you are not just getting a book; you are stepping into the role of a hero in a much larger story—one of empowerment, community transformation, and positive change. The authors have committed to donating 10% of the net sales from this book to the Goal Impact Foundation, a reputable nonprofit organization that works tirelessly to transform communities and empower youth through education and sports programs.

By choosing this book, you become an integral player in a movement that extends far beyond the pages you will turn. Imagine a young person gaining the confidence and skills needed to lead their community toward a brighter future. Your investment helps fund educational and sports programs that nurture these young leaders, directly impacting their lives and the trajectories of their communities.

Every book sold contributes to community-building initiatives that create spaces where youth can learn, play, and grow safely. By choosing this book, you are helping to lay the foundation for healthier, more vibrant communities. As you read about and implement the principles of being a Good Vibe Gangsta, you also fund efforts that sustain global connections and responsibilities. Your actions encourage a broader perspective, making you a global hero in promoting understanding and cooperation.

The stories and strategies in this book are your tools, but the actions you take after turning the last page define the true extent of your heroism. I encourage you to share your story of how this book inspired you to act, to change, and influence. Use your voice on social media, in your community, and among friends to inspire others to join you. Every conversation you start, every post you share, and every recommendation you make expands the ripple effect of your initial heroic act.

The authors cannot do this without you. By joining them on this journey, you demonstrate what it truly means to be a Good Vibe

Gangsta—someone who uses their power for the greater good, leads by example and inspires change through action.

Thank you for being a hero and for choosing to make a difference. Your support is not just appreciated—it is impactful. Together, let us spread the ethos of the Good Vibe Gangsta far and wide, creating ripples of positive change that resonate well beyond our immediate circles.

With all my love and blessings,

Rossi

INTRODUCTION

Welcome, dear reader, to a journey unlike any other—a path that weaves through the terrains of personal growth, social impact, and leadership. You hold in your hands *Awaken Your Good Vibe Gangsta*, a book that challenges conventional notions of success and influence, redefining what it means to be a leader in today's world. This book is not just about achieving personal success; it is about awakening and transforming that success into a bonfire of positivity and inspiration for others.

What is a Good Vibe Gangsta?

The term "Good Vibe Gangsta" might evoke a myriad of images—perhaps a charismatic leader, a community activist, or even a visionary entrepreneur. At its core, a Good Vibe Gangsta is someone who spreads positivity and good vibes, influencing their surroundings not just through words, but through consistent, impactful actions. They are individuals who awaken their personal power and influence to create environments where positivity thrives and where people feel empowered and uplifted.

The Genesis of the Concept

The concept of Good Vibe Gangsta was not born in isolation but was inspired by a brilliant moment of realization and shared experience. The seeds were sown during a particularly stirring event—a historic commencement ceremony at Texas Lutheran University (TLU). On this important day, thousands of individuals gathered, radiating the collective anticipation and exhilaration of a commencement ceremony. Among them was Joey, a TLU alumnus from the class of 2003, who took the stage not just as a keynote speaker but as a visionary entrepreneur, returning to his alma mater to ignite a spark among the new graduates as the youngest alumnus to ever have such an honor.

Joey's speech, later known as the inspirational *'Afford To Care' Commencement Speech*, deeply connected with everyone in attendance. It was a clarion call to the graduates to awaken and adopt a mindset that transcends traditional measures of success. The speech emphasized the importance of caring—caring for one's personal growth, for others, and for the community at large. This philosophy of 'Afford To Care' encapsulates the essence of being proactive, compassionate, and genuinely engaged with the world—principles that are central to the ethos of a Good Vibe Gangsta.

Accompanying Joey was his brother Jimmy, a TLU alumnus from the class of 2006, capturing this significant moment through his lens as a professional photographer and videographer. Together, they documented not only a memorable speech but also a launching point for a concept that would later evolve into this book. Their teamwork and shared experiences as international entrepreneurs and global humanitarians provided them with a unique perspective, deeply ingrained with philanthropic principles and a strong appreciation for diverse backgrounds.

Both Jimmy and Joey have commanded the global stage with an intricate understanding of multicultural environments, spurred by their dual citizenship in the United States and Guatemala, and their fluency in multiple languages. Their experiences have reinforced the belief that understanding and appreciating diverse viewpoints, languages, and artistic expressions—such as soccer and Bosa Nova music, or the arts of Capoeira and Flamenco—enrich one's ability to influence positively and broadly.

Joey's quote, "Education is a lifelong process, and it is imperative to continually gain knowledge as if your journey is eternal," encapsulates their approach to life and leadership. This philosophy of continuous learning and growth is what they aimed to share through the 'Afford To Care' philosophy, urging everyone to see education not just as a formal process but as an endless journey of personal and collective enlightenment.

From this rich mosaic of experiences and the inspiring foundation laid during the commencement speech, the concept of Good Vibe Gangsta took shape. It is more than just a set of actions; it is a way of life that champions positivity, resilience, and the impactful power of caring. This book is an extension of that speech and those principles, aimed at empowering you to live boldly, care deeply, and inspire others to do the same. Through this book, we hope to provide a roadmap for anyone eager to make a significant and positive impact in their personal and professional lives.

Scan the QR code below to watch the historic commencement speech.

If you are unable to access the content with the QR code shared above, please write to support@goodvibegangsta.com.

Purpose of the Book

This book is crafted to guide you on how to embody the essence of a Good Vibe Gangsta. It is not merely about adopting a cheerful outlook but about awakening and integrating seven transformative principles that will enable you to lead, inspire, and influence more effectively. These principles are derived from a blend of personal experiences, psychological research, and timeless wisdom that resonates with anyone looking to make a meaningful impact on both their lives and the lives of those around them.

What You Will Gain

By engaging with this book, you will:

1. Awaken the Power of Positive Influence: Learn how your everyday actions and decisions can significantly influence your personal and professional circles.

2. Build Resilience: Understand how to harness personal setbacks and challenges as opportunities for growth and leadership.
3. Develop Genuine Connections: Acquire skills to create and sustain relationships that are both empowering and supportive.
4. Promote a Culture of Positivity: Gain insights into how you can cultivate an environment that encourages creativity, transformation, and genuine happiness.
5. Achieve Personal and Professional Growth: Discover how living as a Good Vibe Gangsta can lead to significant personal changes and accelerate your chosen pathway.

Good Vibe Gangsta in Action: Supporting the Goal Impact Foundation (GIF)

Empowering Youth and Communities Through Your Investment

As you awaken and embark on this journey with the book, your investment does more than just offer you a guide to personal and professional growth. It directly supports a cause that embodies the very essence of the Good Vibe Gangsta spirit—empowering young minds and communities. We are committed to donating 10% of the net sales from this book to GIF, a reputable non-profit organization dedicated to transforming lives through the power of education and sports programs.

Learn more at: goalimpact.org.

Why Your Investment Matters

By choosing to invest in this book, you play a major role in nurturing the next generation of leaders and innovators. Each investment helps lower barriers to education and sports opportunities for youth, enabling them to unlock and reach their full potential.

Here is what your investment helps achieve:

- Access to Sports: Your support aids in providing youth with the opportunity to engage in sports, which teaches teamwork, discipline, and leadership—skills vital for both personal and community growth.
- STEAM Education: Contributions from this book help develop and implement a STEAM curriculum that prepares young individuals in science, technology, engineering, arts, and mathematics, equipping them with the skills needed for the challenges of tomorrow.
- Scholarships: A portion of the proceeds goes toward scholarships that make higher education more accessible, empowering young minds to pursue their dreams and contribute productively to society.
- Amateur Sports Competitions: By supporting GIF, you help develop and administer sporting events that not only provide a platform for youth to excel but also have a positive economic impact on local communities.

A Case Study in Action: The Impact of Good Vibe Gangsta and Goal Impact Foundation (GIF)

Affiliating with GIF aligns perfectly with the Good Vibe Gangsta philosophy, as both share a common mission: to uplift and transform communities through proactive involvement and education. This collaboration is a living example of how the principles outlined in our book can translate into tangible actions that have a real-world impact.

The Good Vibe Gangsta philosophy is not just about self-improvement; it is about using the skills and positivity we cultivate within ourselves to make a difference in the wider world. By supporting GIF, we extend the reach of our positive influence, turning the personal development of our readers into community development, thus enriching lives beyond the pages of our book.

Your Role in a Larger Movement

When you invest in *Awaken Your Good Vibe Gangsta*, you are not just purchasing a book; you are joining a movement. A movement that champions the power of education, the discipline of sports, and the impact of community support. Your involvement perpetuates personal growth, extending into the broader mission of empowering the leaders of tomorrow. Through your investment, you become a part of a larger story—a story of community, support, and the relentless pursuit of positivity and empowerment.

This is the Good Vibe Gangsta way: leveraging our collective strengths to stimulate an environment where every individual can shine. Together, we can create a legacy that exceeds individual success, crafting a world where we all thrive together. Join us in making this vision a reality, one book, one reader, and one community at a time.

Navigating the Book

Each chapter of the book dives into one of the seven principles, starting with embracing your youthful energy, pursuing your calling with unwavering passion, and learning from failures. We will share narratives, both personal and from others who have walked this path, to illustrate how these principles manifest in real life. Along with these stories, practical advice and chapter summaries will help you apply these principles to your daily life, ensuring the wisdom imparted is not just theoretical but immediately actionable.

Invitation to the Reader

We invite you to approach this book not just as a reader but as an active participant in a movement toward a more positive and proactive society. Whether you are a professional stepping into a leadership role, an entrepreneur crafting a new venture, or simply someone who wishes to have a more meaningful impact on your community, these pages will offer you valuable insights and tools.

In conclusion, as you awaken and embark on this journey with us, remember that each page is a step toward becoming not just a leader but an advocate of positive change—the epitome of a Good Vibe Gangsta. Your journey towards influencing the world in a positive way starts now. Let us begin!

CHAPTER 1
Maintain Youthful Energy

Introduction

Having a youthful spirit throughout life is like holding a lantern against the night, illuminating new opportunities and paths. This energy is not limited to the young; it is a vibrant, potent spirit available to everyone, regardless of their age. It is about adopting a mindset that is profoundly hopeful, insatiably curious, and always open to new experiences.

Youthful energy is a powerful catalyst for change, both personally and professionally. It is more than just a way of thinking. It motivates us to explore, create, and question the status quo, pushing us to set lofty goals and stretch the bounds of what is possible. In a world that frequently values experience and prudence, the energy and boldness of a young spirit can be like a breath of fresh air, reviving stale environments and breathing new life into worn-out systems.

However, it is not always simple to seize this kind of energy. The obligations and everyday grind of life can stifle our natural spirit of exploration and curiosity as we grow older. We develop risk aversion, often choosing the easy route because it is dependable and comfortable. But what if the secret to realizing our greatest potential lies in regaining this carefree energy? What if it led to more creative and prosperous endeavors, as well as a more content personal life?

We will examine the nature of youthful energy in this chapter and talk about useful strategies to use it to your advantage. We will track how maintaining this energy can change the way you confront obstacles, build your resilience, and enable you to live a fulfilling life full of accomplishments. We will also discuss the practical advantages of maintaining this spirit, including how it may keep you physically and psychologically healthy and why it is required for long-term success in a world that is constantly changing.

By the end of this chapter, you will have a better understanding of how to maintain and nurture that youthful vitality, helping you reach your goals at any age. Let us rediscover the significance of living with a youthful spirit and explore how it can illuminate our paths to both professional and personal success.

The Essence of Youthful Energy

What is Youthful Energy?

Youthful energy is fundamentally defined as an unwavering enthusiasm for life. It is a revitalizing force that drives us to passionately pursue our interests. This energy can be developed by anyone who wishes to do so; it is not only the preserve of the young. Youthful energy is characterized by exuberance, bravery, and a never-ending curiosity about the world and our place in it.

Vitality and Vibrancy

Youthful energy is vibrant, permeating every action and inspiring purposeful motion rather than mere movement. This vitality pushes people to innovate, step outside their comfort zones, and see opportunities where others see barriers. It is about being spirited enough to greet life each day with a new outlook and be prepared to face obstacles with a grin.

Endless Curiosity

Curiosity is a vital component of youthful vitality. It is an active, compelling pursuit of information and understanding, rather than just a passive curiosity about the world around us. People who are curious challenge the existing quo, look for novel experiences, and are ever-observant. This unwavering quest for knowledge keeps the intellect active and the soul bright, advancing both professional and personal growth.

Resilience and Flexibility

Resilience is boosted by youthful vitality. Those who are open to this energy are more willing to adjust to changing circumstances and recover from setbacks more quickly because they are optimistic and have a can-do attitude. In the fast-paced world of today, where adaptation is the difference between success and failure, resilience is necessary. Young people's adaptable energy enables them to face life's challenges head-on with dignity and resolve.

Fearlessness and Risk Taking

Fearlessness is another quality that sets youthful energy apart. This implies measured daring to take intentional risks with the potential to yield significant returns, rather than recklessness. In this sense, being fearless is trying new things, pushing outside of your comfort zone, and not being scared to fail. It all comes down to having the courage to push limits in both one's personal and professional life and having faith in one's own talents.

Enthusiasm and Passion

Lastly, youthful energy is characterized by contagious excitement and a deep-seated passion for endeavors. This excitement is not flimsy; rather, it is a deep involvement with life's endeavors that uplifts and inspires others. Similarly, passion is a persistent, enthusiastic interest that propels people to succeed in their undertakings; it is not transient. Enthusiasm and passion work together to produce a potent synergy that inspires and uplifts those around it in addition to igniting personal goals.

Harnessing Youthful Energy

Embracing youthful energy involves actively incorporating these attributes into all facets of life, not just feeling young. It involves practicing fearlessness, building resilience, encouraging curiosity, and leading an enthusiastic and passionate life. People can live richer, more fulfilling lives and encourage others to do the same by modeling these qualities.

In the sections that follow, we will look at how to keep these aspects of youth alive in everyday life and make sure they become a transforming force for both career and personal development. You can genuinely change the world and enter a realm of limitless possibilities by understanding and harnessing this energy.

Harnessing Youthful Optimism

Cultivating an Optimistic Mindset

Youthful optimism is an intentional perspective that can be developed and used to drive both personal and professional growth, rather than just a passing emotion. This kind of optimism is defined by a broad sense of expectation that good things will occur and a conviction that efforts will pay off. It promotes an outlook that is more focused on opportunities than limitations, which strengthens tenacity and fortitude in the face of difficulties.

The Power of Positive Expectations

Our expectations of the world and ourselves are the first steps toward optimism. Optimists naturally gravitate toward solutions because they expect good outcomes and see opportunities for growth and achievement in every obstacle. This optimistic expectation serves as a self-fulfilling prophesy, encouraging people to work harder and persevere in the face of difficulty, which frequently results in better outcomes.

Building a Habit of Positive Thinking

Creating habits that support positive thinking is crucial to capturing youthful optimism. This can be accomplished by using techniques like:

1. Gratitude: Regularly reflecting on and being grateful for what you have helps shift attention from what you lack and promotes optimism.
2. Affirmations: Reaffirming oneself with positive affirmations can help remodel mental patterns and increase the naturalness of an optimistic viewpoint.
3. Visualizing Success: By envisioning positive results, one can prime one's mind to pursue objectives with confidence and zeal, strengthening one's positive outlook.

Challenging Negative Thought Patterns

Being optimistic involves controlling and resisting pessimistic thoughts that sour judgment and depress morale. It entails identifying when you are thinking negatively and purposefully refuting these thoughts with examples of previous accomplishments and potential solutions. Particularly successful are methods like cognitive restructuring, which involve methodically challenging negative thoughts and substituting them with more realistic, upbeat ones.

Learning from Setbacks

In the context of youthful vitality, true optimism also entails a strong reaction to adversity. Rather than seeing setbacks as a reflection of their shortcomings, optimists view them as isolated events and opportunities for growth. Even in the face of challenges, they can sustain their motivation and momentum because of this viewpoint. Using youthful optimism requires taking what you have learned from each experience and using it to go forward with fresh perspective.

Optimism and Risk-Taking

An optimistic outlook encourages taking assumed risks. Faith and favorable results diminishes the anxiety of venturing into uncharted territory or attempting new experiences. With an optimistic outlook, this confidence can inspire the pursuit of novel ideas and uncharted territory that would have appeared too daunting otherwise.

Sustaining Optimism Over Time

Sustaining youthful optimism over time requires deliberate effort. It entails consistently maintaining a cheerful atmosphere, actively seeking out and surrounding oneself with fellow optimists, and routinely partaking in activities that support an optimistic viewpoint. Additionally, maintaining this energy across various stages of life requires remaining adaptable and adjusting to changing situations without losing the vital hopeful nature.

Conclusion

Developing a mindset that consistently looks for the bright side, takes lessons from every circumstance, and utilizes positivity as a tool for development and success is what it means to actively cultivate young optimism. It goes further than simply hoping for the best. Maintaining a positive mindset gives you a powerful tool that supports your goals, strengthens your resilience, and uplifts people around you. We will look at how to incorporate and use this optimism in meaningful, useful ways in both the personal and professional spheres in the following sections.

Cultivating Curiosity and Continuous Learning

Embracing a Lifelong Learning Attitude

Curiosity drives intellectual accomplishment and personal development. It is the continuous search for information that not only broadens our comprehension of the world but also enriches our engagement with it. It is impossible to overestimate the significance of developing curiosity and a dedication to lifelong learning in a world that is continuously changing. These characteristics are needful to youthful vitality because they bolster creativity and preserve the spirit of discovery.

The Benefits of Curiosity

A curious mind promotes an active lifestyle rather than a passive one. As inquisitive people are more inclined to question assumptions, seek out fresh perspectives on issues, and challenge established notions, curiosity cultivates better invention, creativity, and problem-solving abilities. By keeping an open mind, you can keep discovering new possibilities, viewpoints, and ideas, giving yourself every day the possibility to develop.

Strategies for Cultivating Curiosity

- Ask Questions: Encourage yourself to ask more questions in all facets of your life to cultivate curiosity. In meetings, seminars, or reading, challenging the current quo can result in more thorough understanding and creative thinking.
- Expound Broadly: Experiment with topics and pursuits that are outside of your comfort zone to broaden your interests. This could be reading literature in many genres, picking up new interests, or interacting with individuals from various backgrounds.
- Remain Up to Date: Stay abreast of developments, new findings, and fashions in your industry and its allied fields. This maintains your mind active in constant learning and your knowledge base current.

Creating a Learning Environment

You must establish an environment that promotes and enriches continual learning if you are to fully assume it. This includes creating a development mentality, which prioritizes learning over knowing, as well as the psychological environment, which includes setting up a personal learning area.

Utilizing Technology for Learning

Use technology to improve your learning and curiosity. Numerous materials are accessible, ranging from podcasts and instructional apps to webinars and online courses. Accessing a variety of knowledge sources and learning at your own speed and style is made simpler by technology.

The Role of Mindfulness in Learning

By increasing focus and concentration, mindfulness can greatly improve the learning process. By using mindfulness practices, you may increase your awareness and free your mind from distractions, which will improve the effectiveness and efficiency of your learning.

Connecting with Like-Minded Learners

Participate in groups of people who share your interests in education and self-improvement. Through conversations, teamwork, and networking, these relationships can offer inspiration, wisdom, and fresh chances for learning.

Overcoming Barriers to Curiosity

Determine and remove any internal or external obstacles to learning and curiosity. This could entail overcoming failure-related phobias, establishing one's own objectives, or efficiently managing one's time to make time for research and exploration.

Continuous Learning as a Lifestyle

Lastly, incorporate learning into your everyday activities. Make it a way of life, not just a chore or an objective. Every day, schedule time for reading, experimenting, and reflection. Honor the learning process as much as the results, and let your innate curiosity direct your actions.

Conclusion

Sustaining young vitality and assuring ongoing personal and professional development requires nurturing curiosity and making a commitment to lifelong learning. You can improve your capacity to positively impact others in addition to enriching your own life by cultivating a curious mindset and actively participating in learning opportunities. The power of youthful energy can be further harnessed by embracing innovation and taking risks, as we will discuss in the next section.

Taking Risks and Embracing Innovation

Introduction to Risk and Innovation

To advance both personally and professionally, one must be willing to take chances and welcome new ideas. The desire to take risks and try out novel concepts is the foundation of youthful energy. This section dives into the importance of innovation and taking risks as drivers of advancements and clever shifts—two imperative elements of preserving a youthful attitude.

The Essence of Risk-Taking

In the world of youthful energy, risk-taking is perceived as a doorway to possible advantages, even though it is frequently regarded through the lens of prospective loss. Assessing opportunities where potential advantages outweigh potential negatives is a necessary step towards embracing risks. This is not an endorsement of careless behavior, but rather of measured risks that promote development and education.

Benefits of Taking Risks

1. Personal Development: Stepping out of your comfort zone is one of the best strategies to advance yourself.

Every risk has a different obstacle, and overcoming it increases adaptation, resilience, and self-assurance.
2. Professional Advancement: Taking chances pays off in many fields by opening up more options. Risk-takers are usually viewed as leaders who are prepared to launch new initiatives and spur divergence.
3. Finding New chances: A lot of chances are concealed by risk. If you have the courage to take risks, you can discover opportunities that would be hidden in a safety-first mindset.

Cultivating an Innovative Mindset

Risk-taking and reshaping go hand in hand, although innovation is primarily concerned with creativity and the application of novel concepts. It takes an inventive mindset to think outside the box, question received wisdom, and come up with superior solutions to issues that already exist.

Strategies for Embracing Innovation

1. Promote Divergent Thinking: Give yourself permission to think freely and unrestrictedly. This typically results in creative ideas. Hold brainstorming sessions where no concept is off-limits.
2. Encourage Experimentation: Establish a way of life where failure and trial are welcomed, whether in professional or personal endeavors. This may entail allocating funds for experimental initiatives or designating specified times to test out novel concepts.

3. Keep Up with Trends: Keeping up with emerging technology and trends can spark creative thinking and show you what other people in your industry and similar industries are doing creatively.

Managing the Fear of Failure

The fear of failing is a major deterrent to taking chances and embracing inventiveness. Controlling this fear is required and here is how to do it:

- Reframe Failure: See it as a chance for growth and a critical stop along the way to achievement.
- Create Learning Goals: Create learning objectives that emphasize the process and the knowledge you get from it, independent of the result, as opposed to merely creating outcome goals.
- Incremental Risk-Taking: To increase your confidence and comprehension of your risk tolerance, start with lesser risks.

Conclusion

Maintaining our young enthusiasm as we venture into novel experiences and educational prospects necessitates taking chances and welcoming creativity. You can keep developing on the personal and professional fronts by creating an atmosphere that supports these pursuits. We will go into more detail in the following sections about how these components work together to preserve resilience and vitality, which will further emphasize the idea of youthful energy in our lives.

Maintaining Physical Vitality

Introduction to Physical Vitality

Maintaining physical vitality is imperative for maintaining the youthful vigor that drives overall development. It involves more than just maintaining physical health; it also involves taking care of a body that is resilient, energizing, and able to support an involved, active lifestyle. This section investigates the significance of preserving physical vitality and offers doable methods for achieving and preserving it.

The Importance of Physical Health

Physical vitality is the cornerstone of all aspects of life. It improves emotional stability, mental clarity, and general life satisfaction. An active mind and soul are supported by a healthy body, which gives you the energy to take on challenges and bounce back from disappointments more quickly. It plays a vital role in preserving your youthful vitality since it affects your capacity to completely take on the opportunities and responsibilities of life.

Basic Components of Physical Vitality

1. Regular Exercise: Staying physically active is important to preserving health and vigor. It increases energy, strengthens muscles, uplifts mood, and improves cardiovascular health. Wholesome benefits can be obtained by combining cardiovascular, strength training, and flexibility activities.

2. Balanced Nutrition: The body receives vital nutrients from a balanced diet that is high in fruits, vegetables, lean meats, and whole grains. Emotional and cognitive health are impacted by proper nutrition in addition to physical health.
3. Enough Sleep: Good sleep is just as vital as a healthy diet and regular exercise. It enables the mind and body to heal and renew themselves. A regular sleep schedule can improve general health and boost performance and attentiveness during the day.

Strategies for Enhancing Physical Vitality

- Establish a Routine: Choose an exercise regimen that works for your tastes and way of life, then stay with it. Regular exercise is indispensable, whether it is yoga, running, working out at the gym, or participating in sports.
- Arrange Nutritious Meals: Making a meal plan can assist in guaranteeing that you eat a balanced diet all week long. To resist the temptation of choosing less healthy options, think about preparing meals ahead of time.
- Prioritize Sleep: Establish a nightly schedule that promotes healthy sleeping habits. This could entail reducing screen time, winding down before bed, and setting up a cozy sleeping space.

Incorporating Mindfulness and Well-being Practices

Holistic activities like mindfulness and meditation, which lower stress and improve general well-being, can greatly contribute to physical vitality in addition to exercise, diet, and sleep. Frequent practice helps enrich mental well-being, which strengthens physical well-being.

Challenges to Maintaining Physical Vitality

- Hectic Schedules: Having a hectic schedule might make it difficult to find time for healthy eating and exercise. It is critical to consider these tasks as necessary rather than optional.
- Aging: As we become older, our bodies require different things, and physical exercise gets harder. It is critical to modify your health regimens to account for these shifts.

Overcoming Barriers

- Establish Realistic Goals: Begin with attainable objectives that inspire you rather than debilitate you.
- Seek Professional Advice: Personalized advice on optimizing your health regimen can be obtained by consulting with fitness and nutrition specialists.
- Make Use of Technology: Health apps and fitness monitors can help you stay motivated and measure your progress.

Conclusion

Keeping your body healthy is critical to keeping the youthful energy that makes life meaningful. Better health, more energy, and an overall sense of well-being are the benefits that make maintaining a healthy lifestyle worthwhile. By taking proactive measures to care for your body, you ensure that it remains a reliable and strong partner on your life's journey.

Building Resilience Through Enthusiasm

Introduction to Resilience and Enthusiasm

Sustained success and personal development are largely dependent on resilience—the capacity to overcome obstacles, adjust to change, and persevere in the face of difficulty. A passionate engagement with life is the hallmark of enthusiasm, which serves as a potent fuel source for resilience. It not only increases your ability to overcome obstacles but also adds delight and satisfaction to everyday events, making the trip just as worthwhile as the destination.

The Role of Enthusiasm in Resilience

Enthusiasm turns obstacles into opportunities and failures into teaching moments. You are more likely to overcome obstacles when you approach life with enthusiasm because you are motivated by the excitement of participation and keep your eyes on the good things in life. This upbeat attitude is contagious, frequently influencing others and harboring an atmosphere that strengthens resilience as a group.

Cultivating Enthusiasm

1. Discover Your Passion: Exuberance is naturally enhanced when you engage in activities you are passionate about. Determine what motivates and excites you, then incorporate more of these things into your everyday life.

2. Make Inspiring Goals: You can maintain your excitement by setting goals that thrill and inspire you. These objectives ought to be difficult yet doable, in line with your interests, and significant enough to inspire perseverance.
3. Honor Little Victories: Acknowledging and applauding any accomplishment, no matter how modest, will lift your emotions and maintain your zeal. This exercise accentuates the benefits of your work and promotes a positive outlook.

Maintaining Enthusiasm in Adverse Situations

- Positive Framing: Try to frame difficulties in a positive light. Pay attention to what you may learn from the event and how it advances your objectives.
- Stay Connected: You can keep your enthusiasm going by keeping close relationships with positive and encouraging people. Positive reinforcement from others can strengthen your own and give you both a lift when things are hard.
- Appreciate the Chance of Change: You may keep your enthusiasm and receptivity to new experiences alive if you see change as a chance for personal development rather than as a threat.

Linking Enthusiasm to Everyday Tasks

You can tackle even mundane chores with passion if you locate components of them that interest you or relate them to your larger aspirations. This could imply:

- Integrating Creativity: To make mundane activities more pleasurable, come up with inventive ways to complete them.
- Mindfulness in Action: By giving your whole attention to the present moment, routine tasks can become more interesting.
- Learning Opportunities: View every work as an opportunity to pick up new knowledge, which will help you stay energetic and mentally active.

Building a Resilient Mindset Through Enthusiasm

Failures do not break a peppy spirit strengthened by zeal. Rather, it looks for reasons to carry on and chances to change. This includes:

- Building Grit: Enthusiasm for the work or goal strengthens grit, which is the mix of passion and tenacity that is necessary for long-term goals.
- Adaptive Thinking: Apply your passion for creativity and problem-solving to develop the ability to think flexibly and change tactics when confronted with challenges.

Conclusion

Developing resilience through enthusiasm involves more than just maintaining an optimistic outlook: it requires fully embracing life's endeavors and finding joy in the process. By cultivating enthusiasm, you may build resilience, making you more capable of overcoming obstacles in life and more likely to reach your objectives with a sense of contentment and satisfaction. This upbeat attitude not only encourages personal development but also uplifts those around you, amplifying the effect of your contagious energy.

Case Studies: Youthful Energy in Action

In this section, the experiences of people who embody the Good Vibe Gangsta spirit allow us to prowl the transforming potential of youthful energy in action. In this book we discuss many principles, and each story not only demonstrates how to put these principles into practice but also showcases the incredible results that can happen when someone steps outside the norm.

Why These Examples Matter

Significant changes often result from critical moments where risk takes on new significance in the path of personal and professional growth. By looking at actual cases, we provide you with more than just ideas—we give you concrete evidence of how taking chances and encouraging creativity can result in noteworthy accomplishments. The following makes these tales compulsory:

1. Show Feasibility: You can feel more certain that taking a leap of faith is not only conceivable but can also be quite gratifying when you observe how others have managed similar situations.
2. Emphasize Dissimilar Approaches: Every narrative offers a different viewpoint on how to incorporate taking chances and creative problem-solving into your daily life. This variety aids in the discovery of tactics that suit both your personal and professional situation.

3. Promote Boldness: Seeing the accomplishments of others can inspire you to follow your own gut feelings and affirm your inner Good Vibe Gangsta.
4. Offer Learning Opportunities: Every example covers both the triumphs, and the difficulties faced along the route. These observations can be very helpful to you in preparing for and overcoming similar obstacles on your path.
5. Encourage a Community of Inspiration: Readers who share these experiences get to know one another better and are inspired to work together for personal development and influence.

Our goal in sharing these real-world examples is to show how the concepts covered in this book may be put into practice while also encouraging you to do the same in your own life. While perusing these narratives, contemplate how you might apply the acquired knowledge to your everyday routines to accelerate your development into an authentic Good Vibe Gangsta.

Real-Life Examples of 'Maintain Youthful Energy'

Let us look at the first of this book's many motivational case studies.

Liz Peters: A Fusion of Strength, Flexibility, and Vivid Energy

Liz, affectionately known as 'Peaches,' symbolizes the essence of youthful energy with her vivacious and spirited approach to fitness and life. She is a Manager at The Union Fitness & Fun and an expert in a variety of disciplines. These include functional fitness, strength training, USAW sports performance coaching, and an array of yoga and pilates certifications like Bikram yoga, inferno hot pilates, mat pilates, and power yoga.

Peaches' journey into the world of athletics began in her early years, showcasing a natural aptitude in soccer, which paved the way for her lifelong passion for fitness. Her adventure took a turn in 2002 when she was introduced to Bikram Yoga. After four years of nurturing a love/hate relationship with the discipline, Peaches' commitment to deepening her understanding of the body's needs led her to complete a rigorous Bikram Yoga Teacher Training.

The real turning point came when Liz discovered functional fitness training and experienced an epiphany about her professional path. She realized her calling was not just in practicing these disciplines but in sharing her extensive knowledge of how strength and flexibility synergize to upgrade overall health. Liz's philosophy centers on empowering others to let loose their potential by embracing both the vigor of functional fitness training and the poise of yoga, nurturing a balanced approach to physical wellness.

When she is not coaching or managing her fitness studio, Liz can be found indulging in her love for crafting the perfect mug cake, diving into episodes of 'Below Deck,' or unraveling the complexities of the latest true crime mysteries. Her personal motto, 'pobody's nerfect,' reflects her down-to-earth personality and her belief in embracing imperfections while striving for personal growth.

Liz's energetic lifestyle and varied expertise make her an exemplary figure in this book. Her story illustrates the power of embracing youthful energy, taking risks, and innovating across different aspects of life and work. Through her example, you can learn the importance of integrating multifaceted skills and passions to lead a fulfilling and impactful life, truly awakening your Good Vibe Gangsta within.

We had the honor of having a Q&A session with Liz about the book and here is what she had to say.

Q1: Can you describe what youthful energy means to you and how it has influenced your life?

A1: "Youthful energy, to me, represents a vigorous, boundless enthusiasm and an eagerness to experiment and experience life fully. This kind of energy drives curiosity and fearlessness in trying new things, whether it is a new fitness regimen at the gym, a fresh recipe in the kitchen, or a daring travel adventure.

In my life, this energy has been a major influence in advancing a willingness to innovate and adapt, peculiarly in managing at The Union. It is about maintaining that spirited optimism in both personal and professional environments, constantly encouraging others to push their limits and discover their potential. This energy is infectious and fundamental in creating a motivating atmosphere, encouraging everyone around to stay young at heart, no matter their age."

Q2: How has practicing mindfulness impacted your capacity to embrace and use your youthful energy?

A2: "Practicing mindfulness has deeply enriched my ability to harness and channel youthful energy. By staying present and aware, I have learned to focus this energy more effectively, turning enthusiasm into productivity and creativity. In both management and personal wellness, mindfulness helps recognize the body and mind's needs, ensuring that this vital energy is used positively rather than leading to burnout.

Moreover, mindfulness builds resilience, allowing me to meet challenges with a clear head and a calm spirit, preserving that youthful spark even in stressful situations. It encourages a balanced approach to life, where energy is sustained through intentional rest and rejuvenation, enhancing my ability to inspire and lead others effectively."

Q3: Can you share a specific instance where mindfulness helped you overcome a challenge that required a lot of youthful energy and resilience?

A3: "Absolutely! One specific instance that comes to mind was when we decided to introduce a new fitness program at The Union Fitness and Fun. The program was quite innovative and demanding, combining elements of high-intensity interval training with a leveling method. The challenge was not just the physical aspect but also ensuring our members felt engaged and supported through this change.

During this period, I practiced mindfulness to maintain clarity and focus among the intense activity and mixed feedback. Each morning, I took time for a short meditation and set intentions for the day, reminding myself to stay patient and open to member responses. This practice helped me stay grounded and empathetic, allowing me to address concerns with calmness and encouraging team members effectively.

Thanks to this mindful approach, I was able to lead with enthusiasm and resilience, ensuring the program's successful implementation and helping our members adapt positively to the new challenge. It turned out to be a remarkable success, adding an electrifying energy to our community."

Q4: What advice would you give to other individuals looking to tap into their youthful energy to pursue their passions?

A4: "To anyone looking to tap into their youthful energy to pursue their passions, I would recommend a few crucial strategies:

1. Stay Curious: Always be willing to learn and try new things. This keeps your mind engaged and your spirit lively, just like when you were younger, and everything was new.
2. Tackle Challenges: View challenges as opportunities to gain experience rather than obstacles. This mindset can invigorate you and inject a dose of youthful enthusiasm into your projects.
3. Balance Energy with Rest: It is paramount to manage your energy wisely. High energy parallels are great, but sustainable success requires periods of rest and reflection to recharge.
4. Connect with Like-minded Individuals: Surround yourself with people who share your passion and enthusiasm. Their energy can be contagious and provide a great motivational boost.
5. Practice Mindfulness: This helps in maintaining a clear focus and managing stress, ensuring that your energy is directed constructively towards your passions.

Using these strategies, you can channel your youthful energy effectively to not only pursue your passions but also enjoy every step of the journey."

Q5: Looking forward, how do you plan to keep this youthful spirit alive as you continue your trips around the sun?

A5: "Looking forward, my plan to keep the youthful spirit alive involves a few indispensable commitments:

1. Continuous Learning: I aim to stay curious and open-minded, learning new skills and exploring new ideas. This keeps the mind sharp and the spirit young.
2. Physical Wellness: Maintaining a regular workout routine, which is needed for both physical and mental health. Activities like yoga and functional fitness training not only keep the body in shape but also endorphins high, fueling a youthful zest for life.
3. Community Engagement: Staying connected with a community that shares a vivacious and positive outlook helps reinforce my own energy and enthusiasm.
4. Mindfulness Practice: Continuing my mindfulness practices will be fundamental. This helps in managing stress and maintaining mental clarity, allowing me to appreciate and enjoy every moment fully.
5. Embracing Change: Being open to change and willing to adapt is focal. It is about seeing change as an exciting opportunity rather than something to fear.

By sticking to these principles, I am confident that I can maintain and celebrate a youthful spirit, no matter how many more trips around the sun I take."

Conclusion

Liz Peters is a perfect example of how having a lively attitude and embracing one's passions can lead to both professional and personal success. Her path from the soccer fields to the yoga mat and the challenging functional fitness training arenas demonstrates her dedication to encouraging strength and well-being in all facets of life. Liz is a living example of the transformational potential of living fearlessly and having a great sense of compassion. She inspires and empowers others through her fitness programs and personal example. Her narrative inspires us all to pursue our passions with delight and to build resilience and good health, demonstrating that individual development and social influence may coexist peacefully.

Now let us review another emotive case study by one of this book's authors.

Jimmy: Collegiate Men's Soccer Coach & Digital Marketer

Jimmy's journey as an Assistant Coach for the Men's Soccer team at Texas Lutheran University (TLU) encapsulates the essence of maintaining youthful energy which he is grateful for due to his healthy relationship with Eddie Salazar, the tenured Head Coach. This relationship, born during their college days as teammates, exemplifies another indispensable aspect of being a Good Vibe Gangsta—maintaining and championing positive relationships.

Jimmy's foresight in establishing and managing social media platforms for the TLU Men's Soccer program has revolutionized the way the team connects with the community and promotes their activities. By tapping into the power of digital marketing, Jimmy has not only broadened the reach and visibility of the program but also created an activated online community that engages students, alumni, and soccer enthusiasts alike.

This initiative showcases Jimmy's commitment to continuously developing his professional skills and stay in tune with the preferences and communication styles of younger generations. His proactive approach to leveraging technology for community building and promotion exemplifies a primary element of the Good Vibe Gangsta ethos—remaining open-minded and adaptable to new methods.

Furthermore, his active management of these platforms ensures that they are not just promotional tools but vital spaces for interaction, celebration, and motivation. This strategic use of digital media has significantly sharpened the program's ability to attract new talents, engage with fans, and keep the soccer community informed and excited about their achievements and events.

Jimmy's role in digitalizing the TLU Men's Soccer program's presence not only keeps the team current and relevant but also reflects his understanding of the importance of evolving with the times. This adaptation has not just made a positive impact on the program but also serves as an inspiring model for the student-athletes, teaching them the value of embracing new challenges and continuously learning—core principles of the Good Vibe Gangsta philosophy.

Here are some of Jimmy's chief insights that might help you if you are creating and managing social media and digital marketing for a sports team or organization:

1. Understand Your Audience: Know who your fans are, what they like, and when they are most active online.

Adapting content to match the interests and engagement patterns of your audience can significantly increase its impact.
2. Consistency is Paramount: Regular updates keep the audience engaged and informed. Establish a consistent posting schedule to maintain visibility and relevance in your followers' feeds.
3. Engage, Don't Just Broadcast: Social media is a two-way street. Engage with your audience by responding to comments, asking questions, and participating in community discussions. This builds a stronger connection with your fans.
4. Use Visuals Effectively: High-quality images, videos, and graphics are momentous in sports marketing. They capture attention more effectively than text alone and can channel the excitement of the game.
5. Highlight Behind-the-Scenes: Fans love exclusive, behind-the-scenes content. Sharing photos and stories from practices, locker rooms, or team travel can give fans a closer look at the team's personality.
6. Leverage Player Profiles: Feature stories and profiles of players to personalize the team. Fans appreciate knowing more about the athletes they support, both on and off the field.
7. Monitor and Adapt: Use analytics tools to track the performance of your posts and campaigns. Understanding what works and what does not allows you to refine your strategy over time.

8. Promote Across Multiple Channels: Utilize a variety of social media platforms to reach different segments of your audience. Each platform has unique features and demographics, so modify your content accordingly.
9. Create Campaigns for Special Events: Build excitement and engagement with special campaigns for season openers, playoffs, or rival games. These can include countdowns, giveaways, or live updates.
10. Stay Updated on Digital Trends: The digital environment is constantly changing. Staying abreast of new tools, platforms, and trends in social media can help you maintain an advanced presence.

Over the years, Jimmy and Eddie have cultivated a bond that transcends their past as teammates to form the cornerstone of the soccer program's traditions. Their shared history provides a solid foundation of trust and mutual respect, enabling them to collaborate effectively and support each other in developing the soccer program. Their relationship showcases the power of positive connections and how they can influence a community for the better. By maintaining a healthy and supportive relationship, Jimmy and Eddie demonstrate to their student athletes the importance of teamwork, loyalty, and mutual support. These values are integral to the Good Vibe Gangsta philosophy, emphasizing that success is not just about individual achievements but about uplifting each other and growing together.

The enduring partnership between Jimmy and Eddie amplifies the program's vibe, infusing it with energy, understanding, and a shared commitment to excellence. It teaches the student athletes about the significance of maintaining positive relationships throughout their lives, reinforcing that these bonds are as influential to personal and professional success as any skill learned on the field. This narrative not only enriches the coaching dynamic but also solidifies the broader message of the Good Vibe Gangsta ethos, bringing out the recast power of positivity and strong relationships.

Jimmy's legacy-building through the act of giving back to the community and the program that shaped him illustrates the penetrating impact of the Good Vibe Gangsta way. It is not just about achieving personal success but also about inspiring a supportive community where everyone is encouraged to thrive. This legacy of positivity and empowerment is perhaps the most powerful proof to embracing youthful energy, proving that the spirit of giving and mentorship can echo across generations and transform lives.

Conclusion

As we come to the end of this chapter on embracing your youthful energy, keep in mind that the zeal and energy you channel into your work today can help you achieve both professional and personal greatness. Every anecdote and tactic offered here is intended to provoke action as well as inspiration, transforming learnings into routines. With your newfound energy, you are ready to tackle the next chapter, where we will explore how pursuing your calling with unwavering passion is not just fulfilling, but also transformative.

CHAPTER 1 SUMMARY

MAINTAIN YOUTHFUL ENERGY

This chapter inspires you to harness and retain your youthful vigor, using it as a driving force in all aspects of life.

DIAGNOSIS

Many adults lose their youthful energy and curiosity, leading to a stagnant personal and professional life.

PROGNOSIS

Rekindle your youthful spirit by engaging in new experiences, maintaining a curious mindset, and embracing playfulness.

TREATMENT

Actively seek out learning opportunities and engage in activities that challenge you and bring joy.

REQUIREMENTS

Commitment to self-exploration and openness to integrating youthful enthusiasm into daily routines.

NEXT CHAPTER
Pursue Passions

CHAPTER 2

Pursue Passions

Introduction

The idea of following one's passions transcends what is typically thought of as a profession or job. It is a pursuit that aligns closely with one's core desires, skills, and sense of purpose; it offers a route to real fulfillment and a meaningful life rather than merely a way to make ends meet. This chapter encourages you to embark on a profound journey to find and pursue your vocation with tenacity, stressing that doing so is not only a matter of personal preference but also a vital component of leading a fully realized life.

What Does It Mean to Have Passions?

Passions are the most powerful combinations of your innermost desires and strongest traits. They are the things you are 'called' to do; they are so inherently in line with your identity that they feel more like your destiny than a decision. Working from your passions gives you a strong sense of purpose that energizes both yourself and those around you. It imbues each day with vitality and significance and gives your actions purpose and fulfillment.

Why Pursue Passions?

Living true to yourself means pursuing your passions. It allows you to fully express your unique gifts and callings in ways that are intrinsically fulfilling. Additionally, it positions you to significantly impact the world by offering services or producing goods infused with your integrity and vision. In addition to resulting in professional success, this alignment of one's abilities with external demands also brings a deep sense of contentment and satisfaction.

The Journey Ahead

Finding and following your passions is an exciting and challenging journey. Honesty, reflection, and occasionally the courage to venture into the unfamiliar are necessary. This chapter will walk you through this life-changing process and provide you with doable tactics to help you find and follow your true calling with tenacity and fortitude.

This chapter offers a game plan for understanding the fundamental components of a calling and explores ways to align your work life with your passions and core values. You will discover how to set practical goals, adapt to changing conditions, and overcome the inevitable roadblocks that arise in the pursuit of your passions.

Conclusion

As we go into the mechanics of identifying and pursuing your passions with unwavering determination, keep in mind that the purpose of this journey is not only to find the ideal path but also to affirm and discover your true self and the ways in which you can make the greatest impact on the world. This is a demanding but worthwhile endeavor that offers a life filled with passion, purpose, and personal growth. Together, set out on this adventure to discover the means of attaining success and building a deeply meaningful and impactful life.

Understanding Your Passions

Defining a Passion

A passion is a persistent calling and an innate desire to pursue endeavors that align closely with one's identity and core principles. It is a special fusion of your skills, passions, and what the world needs, surpassing conventional job classifications. It is a personal quest that brings happiness and constructively advances society. Understanding your calling means finding the intersections of your innermost passions and talents with opportunities to have a significant impact.

Components of a Passion

1. Calling: The most striking feature of a passion is its calling. It provides the drive and tenacity required to pursue long-term objectives in the face of difficulty. Your calling sustains you when others might give up.

2. Talents and Skills: A genuine passion utilizes your natural abilities and skills. It is critical to recognize your innate talents as well as the skills you have acquired over time. This knowledge enables you to use your skills in the most effective way possible.
3. Values: Your core values, the tenets that guide your choices and behavior, are intimately linked to your passion. Your work feels intrinsically right and satisfying when it aligns with these principles.
4. Contribution: A passion involves a component of contribution. It entails improving the lives of others, whether directly by producing something worthwhile or by motivating change. This outside emphasis strengthens the sense of purpose and keeps motivation high.

Identifying Your Passions

Finding your passions is a journey that requires introspection, experimentation, and self-examination. To help you with this process, follow these steps:

1. Self-Reflection: Take some time to reflect on the moments when you felt most alive and engaged. How did you spend your time? Who were you assisting? What recurring themes can you spot that might indicate your calling?
2. Feedback and Exploration: Without outside perspectives, it can be difficult to recognize our own abilities and capabilities. Ask those who know you well, such mentors, relatives, or friends, for their opinions. They

may be able to reveal aspects of your interests and abilities of which you are unaware.
3. Goals and Principles Alignment: Reflect on your life's most important values and how they could apply to your livelihood or personal endeavors. Determine how you will incorporate your values into your long-term objectives and daily activities.
4. Trial and Error: By experimenting, you can assess your interests and theories related to your calling. This could involve taking on novel tasks, giving back to the community, or shadowing experts in related fields. Every encounter can offer insightful information and serve as a guide to either affirm or change your trajectory.

Living Your Passions

The challenging part of discovering your passions is figuring out how to pursue them daily. This entails setting objectives, making decisions based on your values and passions, and making ongoing adjustments as your understanding of your calling grows.

Conclusion

Discovering and pursuing your passions is one of the most fulfilling journeys you can embark on. It provides a deep sense of fulfillment and purpose, as each step you take has a special meaning. This journey is about creating a life that is truly worth living, not just about attaining success in the traditional sense, as we continue to find out how to pursue this passion with tenacity.

Determine Your Calling

Introduction to Discovering Your Path

One of the most meaningful things you can do in life is probably to determine what your calling is. It requires reflection, observation, and a readiness to put newfound understanding into practice. This process involves not just identifying your strengths but also forming a deep connection with what makes you happy, reflects your values, and contributes to a cause larger than yourself.

Self-Assessment: Understanding Your Strengths and Passions

One of the first steps in discovering your calling is completing a thorough self-evaluation. Exploring your passions, abilities, and interests is part of the process. It can be helpful to identify areas of natural interest to ask reflective questions like "What activities make me lose track of time?" or "What issues am I passionate about?" Further objectivity and clarity can be obtained by using tools such as professional skill assessments and personality tests (e.g., Enneagram, Myers-Briggs, Ikigai).

Feedback and Dialogue: Gaining External Perspectives

Our self-evaluations frequently require the addition of outside viewpoints to be completely encompassing. Talking with close friends, relatives, or mentors who are familiar with your personality and have observed your growth over time can yield a wealth of information. Find out what they think are your strengths and what environments they believe you work best in.

Exploring Your Interests: Trial and Experimentation

Knowing in theory what your potential vocation might be is one thing, but actually experiencing it might confirm or change your course. Engage in activities that allow you to dive deeper into your interests. This could entail beginning side projects that are in line with your selected passions, volunteering in a variety of sectors, or accepting internships. These experiences are vital because they help you better identify your true passions and expose you to the realities of different pathways.

Aligning With Core Values

Your highest ideals should be squared up with your calling. Reflect on your core values and beliefs. Consider creating a personal mission statement that encapsulates your values and goals. Your work will be meaningful and central to your feeling of self and purpose if your path is in line with these ideals.

Looking for Patterns

Look for recurring trends when you experiment, evaluate yourself, receive feedback, and adjust your values. These patterns might indicate a vocation that is a natural fit for you and are signs of your true calling. These could show themselves as recurrent themes in the activities you want to do, the comments you get, or the issues you want to get solved.

Documenting the Journey

It might be quite beneficial to record your findings, ideas, and emotions in a notebook or log during this process. Documenting your journey makes it easier to notice connections you might otherwise overlook, track your progress, and reflect on your experiences. Your documented trip will prove to be an invaluable asset as you proceed and begin to make decisions regarding following your calling.

Conclusion

Finding your calling is a continuous and evolving process. Finding the special junction of your skills, interests, and life's purpose is what really makes you tick. Keep an open mind and be prepared to change course as you go through this process to better understand who you are and the kind of impact you want to make in the world. We will look at goal-setting and practical planning in the upcoming parts to help you fulfill your just realized calling.

The Relentless Pursuit

Introduction to Relentless Pursuit

The process of turning your idea into reality starts as soon as you have determined your calling. The Relentless Pursuit phase is defined by unwavering dedication to reaching your objectives, constant effort, and deliberate action. Through strategic planning, flexibility, and a resilient mindset, you may successfully manage the opportunities and challenges that lie ahead.

Setting Clear and Compelling Goals

The first step in following your calling is to establish clear, measurable, and compelling goals. In addition to being in line with your calling, these objectives ought to be organized in a way that inspires and directs you. Make sure your objectives are Specific, Measurable, Achievable, Relevant and Time-bound by using the SMART criteria. To keep moving forward and monitor progress, divide more ambitious objectives into more manageable milestones.

Developing a Strategic Plan

Create a strategic plan that details the actions required to reach your goals after you have set them. There should be both short-term and long-term goals in this plan. Consider possible roadblocks and devise ways to overcome them. This could entail acquiring new skills, expanding one's professional network, or going back to school. A well-considered strategy serves as a map, guiding your choices and actions toward your main goal.

Continuous Learning and Skill Advancement

Ongoing education is obligatory if you are to follow your purpose with tenacity. Any profession's environment can change quickly, so it is important to stay knowledgeable and proficient. This could be taking workshops, getting further qualifications, or participating in ongoing professional development. Maintaining current knowledge and sharp skills is crucial to staying competitive and productive in your line of work.

Resilience and Adaptability

Any worthwhile endeavor will inevitably encounter difficulties and failures. Gaining resilience, or the capacity to overcome adversity, is major. Develop an attitude that views criticism as valuable feedback for growth and mistakes as learning opportunities. Resilience is correlated with adaptability. When things change or you get more insight into the road you have chosen, be ready to shift course or modify your approach.

Leveraging Networks and Mentors

No endeavor is done alone. Building a strong professional network and finding mentors can help you advance more quickly. Networks help, counsel, and the ability to access opportunities that might not otherwise be available. Mentors assist you in navigating the difficulties of your passage by providing advice and sharing their experiences. Make a conscious effort to find connections that will reinforce your pursuit and support your objectives.

Sustaining Motivation Over Time

It can be difficult to stay highly motivated for extended periods of time, particularly when things are moving slowly or when challenges seem insurmountable. Seek strategies to sustain your motivation, such as setting and celebrating small achievements, maintaining a positive work-life balance, and reminding yourself of the greater goal that drives your efforts.

Persistence Pays Off

Persistence is essential to following your calling with tenacity. There will be moments when only your commitment and unwavering resolve will keep you moving forward. Recall your motivation for beginning this trip and the desired outcome. Being persistent involves more than just obstinately moving forward; it also involves deftly negotiating the way to your objectives and choosing when to adjust and when to push.

Conclusion

Pursuing your calling with tenacity is an invigorating and rewarding experience. It is a dedication to leading an impactful and meaningful life. As you proceed, recollect your objectives, keep learning and adapting, and rely on your network for advice and assistance. This chapter lays the foundation of transforming the pursuit of your calling into your life's work, ensuring that the process is just as fulfilling as achieving the goals themselves.

Making an Impact

Introduction to Making an Impact

Making a difference in the world by working toward your calling is ultimately what it means to follow your calling. Aligning your personal mission with broader societal needs can maximize your contribution to the community while enhancing personal fulfillment.

Coordinating Personal Goals with Societal Needs

It is weighty to match your personal objectives with societal demands if you want to have a genuine impact. This entails comprehending the opportunities and difficulties in your sector of choice and figuring out how your special talents and interests might meet those needs. By doing this, you make sure that your efforts have a positive ripple impact on others in addition to being personally fulfilling.

Contributing to the Community

1. Community Engagement: You can make a bigger impact by actively participating in causes relevant to your calling within the community. Engaging in volunteer work, conducting workshops, or serving on community boards are some of the ways you may put your abilities to use and witness the results of your efforts.
2. Forming Partnerships: You can have a greater influence if you form alliances with groups and people that share your vision. These partnerships can provide access to broader networks, resources, and expertise, enabling you to expand your efforts and reach new audiences.
3. Advocacy and Awareness: Make use of your position and voice to promote causes that are important to your mission. The effects of your individual acts can be multiplied by systemic changes brought about by policy changes and awareness-raising.

Building a Legacy

Making sure that your contributions continue to inspire and impact people long after you are gone is cardinal to leaving a legacy. This includes:

1. Mentorship: You can extend your influence over time by sharing your knowledge and expertise with the next generation. By enabling others to continue your work, mentoring gives you the opportunity to multiply your influence.

2. Sustainable Practices: Create procedures and frameworks that will endure after your personal involvement. This might involve producing books, developing training curricula, or establishing autonomous groups that uphold your values.
3. Recording Your Journey: Maintaining a journal of your approaches, challenges, triumphs, and discoveries can greatly assist others who aspire to emulate you or learn from your experiences.

Measuring Impact

It is critical to have measurement systems in place if you want to understand the full extent and magnitude of your influence. This could entail:

1. Creating Impact Objectives: Setting precise impact objectives will help you concentrate your efforts and measure your progress, much like setting personal and professional goals.
2. Feedback Loops: Getting input from people who are impacted by your work on a regular basis can help you assess your performance and identify areas for improvement.
3. Impact Assessments: Regular reviews and evaluations can assist in measuring your influence, enabling you to modify your tactics and procedures to improve efficacy.

Conclusion

Achieving personal success is only one aspect of making an impact through your vocation; the other is using your skills and passions to change the world for the better and leave a legacy. You can lead a life that is both transforming and meaningful by actively searching out opportunities to give back to the community and concentrating on how your work can help others. This method not only improves your personal life but also fortifies society, leaving a legacy of inspiration and impact.

Real-Life Examples of 'Pursue Passions'

This section traverses the life-changing potential of pursuing your passions via the testimonies of people who personify the Good Vibe Gangsta. Every story demonstrates not only how the principles covered in this book may be put into practice, but also the extraordinary results that can happen when someone is willing to go outside the box.

Lisa Ingle-Stevens: Empowering Through Movement and Leadership

Lisa, a beacon of health, education, and personal growth, embodies the Good Vibe Gangsta ethos through her dedication to empowering others. She is a graduate of Trinity University (TX) and the co-owner of The Union in San Antonio, Texas. As an accomplished yoga and movement instructor, Lisa's journey reflects her passion for teaching and her commitment to lifelong learning and personal development.

Lisa's heartfelt connection with yoga began in 1999 when she attended her first Bikram Yoga class. The immediate impact of this practice sparked a desire not only to endorse yoga personally but to share its inspirational power with others. Her dedication led her to complete the Bikram Yoga Teacher Training Certification in Los Angeles in 2002, marking the start of a lifelong mission to help others heal and thrive through yoga.

In the spring of 2004, Lisa channeled her passion into action by opening her first yoga studio, laying the foundation for what would become a cornerstone of the San Antonio, Texas community's wellness. Under her guidance, The Union expanded to include additional locations, each serving as a hub for health and personal growth.

Lisa's influence extends beyond the yoga mat. She is certified as a 500-RYT through Yoga Alliance and serves on the faculty with Beryl Bender Birch through the Hard & Soft Institute, emphasizing her role not just as a practitioner but also as a mentor and leader in the global yoga community. Her certifications in Leadership Development and her role as a Lightyear Leadership coach further showcase her commitment to fostering leadership skills in others.

In 2019, Lisa co-founded The U Institute, a Leadership and Education learning company dedicated to nurturing lifelong learners and providing them with the physical and mental tools needed to live their best lives. This initiative agrees with her belief in continuous personal growth and her commitment to empowering others to pursue their passions and potential.

Outside the studio and classroom, Lisa's life is filled with the joys of dancing, reading, traveling, and continuous learning. She is married to an incredible man named Kyle, has a beautiful, smart, and funny 11-year-old daughter named Olivia, and feels most at home when she is with her friends, family, and animals (JoJo, Abby, Charlie, and Ginger). Her favorite quote, "Rule #1: Don't hang out with losers," reflects her belief in surrounding oneself with positive influences and aspiring towards greatness in all facets of life.

Lisa is a vivid example of how pursuing one's passions can lead to significant professional achievements and personal satisfaction. Her story is featured in this book to inspire you to take bold steps towards your own dreams, integrate your interests into impactful walks of life, and actively contribute to a positive and effervescent community. Through Lisa's narrative, we see the power of embracing risk, promoting originality, and relentlessly pursuing a path that is both enriching and enlightening.

We had the privilege of having a Q&A session with Lisa about the book, and here is what she had to say.

Q1: What does pursuing your passions mean to you, and how did you identify them?

A1: "I think the word PASSION is often misunderstood. Its origin comes from the Latin root *patior*, which means to suffer or endure. Over the years, it has evolved to include the idea that passion is what sustains you while you are suffering. In my mind, I do not see PASSION as something you pursue. I see it more as something that ignites your natural gifts from within. Our current world is inundated with messaging, and I have often observed both in myself and others, that we are not connected to what truly lights us up from within. We can get so fragmented and disconnected, that we do not even know why we are doing things and how they make us feel. My experience with pursuing my own passions, are that when something matters and allows me to feel as if I have purpose for myself and others, it is not something I have to endure or suffer through, it is also something that reminds me that passion creates energy, light, and choice. When I pursue my passions, I feel illuminated from within, time almost stops, and it creates a magnetic force that inspires others to witness an upward spiral of possibility. When I feel that type of energy or am in the presence of someone else experiencing this, it puts me back into my own orbit for others to always see light where they may think darkness only lives."

Q2: How has integrating mindfulness into your daily routine impacted your professional pursuits?

A2: "The term mindfulness has become increasingly popular over the last decade, yet this concept of being present and in the moment has existed for hundreds of years. One of my mentors and teachers, Beryl Bender Birch, has taught me to pay attention. It is only when we are in the present time that our attention can help us make choices from what is, versus creating narratives and hallucinations in our brains that are not true. Based on my own experiences and practices with mindfulness, it is what allows me to not miss out on what is right in front of me and learn to not fight what is happening in the current moment. In my professional pursuits, there have been so many times over the years as a business owner and boss that I have caught myself living in the past or living in the future because of not wanting something or someone to be a certain way. I have learned what a waste of energy this can be, and it is here where the integration of my mindfulness practices can be so vital to avoid spiraling down and out of control. When I am present, the waves of chaos and instability are so much smaller and allow me to stay true to my purpose in life."

Q3: Can you share an example of a challenge you faced while following your passion and how you used mindfulness to navigate it?

A3: "In 1999, I found the practice of yoga. From the very first class, I knew that I wanted to open a yoga studio one day, creating a home and place for people to put themselves back together time and time again, both physically and mentally. This pursuit, which was entirely led by my passions for healing, illumination, and community, proved to be much harder than I had thought. As a young 22-year-old Hispanic woman, I encountered many "NO's." Trying to find a bank that would give my business partner and I a loan or a real estate owner who would rent us a space almost became impossible. In these moments of resistance, I had to harness mindfulness and stay focused on the vision of what I knew was absolutely possible. The fire inside of me to create The Union got bigger and bigger and by staying committed to my passion and purpose, we eventually found and attracted the people who were willing to take a chance on our concept. I have often found that when things do not work out smoothly or quickly, this is where the true test and learning occur for all of us. There is something to learn when we face challenges and if in these moments we choose to turn to negativity or lose hope, we begin to create this as a pattern in our lives which can permanently affect how we handle obstacles that are put in our way. We can choose when these moments arise in our path, which we all will experience at some point, to stay committed to our passion and not allow others' opinions to allow us to collapse and feel small."

Q4: What advice would you give to someone who is struggling to align their career with their passions?

A4: "Over the years I have heard people say that you should never make your passion your career yet, I have so many living examples that if certain people had not made their passion their career the world would have missed out. I feel we all have blind spots, and where this can be tricky when we are aligning our passion to our career, is not being open to other people's points of views or suggestions. Our passion cannot be taken from us, it can only be dimmed if we allow it. If we become too narrow minded to how things are supposed to look when we are pursuing our passion within a career, it can turn into a pursuit of proving others wrong, versus a pursuit of growth and learning to get us each where we need to be, not where we want to be. We need to always hold our vision clearly in our mind, yet sometimes the path we are headed is not a straight or direct line. Through some of my own struggles, I have personally experienced growth that only added to my passion and helped guide my choices in a much better way. Roadblocks and stop signs are opportunities for us all to see where we are headed and if we are going in the right direction."

Q5: Looking ahead, how do you plan to continue integrating your passions and mindfulness with your career and business goals?

A5: "I believe that integrating your passion and mindfulness requires daily and consistent practice and it is there where our goals can flourish. We must be willing to stay in the uncomfortable and not always be in the pursuit of completion and understanding. As humans, we can quickly give in to our instincts, not wanting to be in the unknown and feeling limited with our time. However, when we are present in the moment, we can learn more about who we are and what we want to pursue, as well as learn from our previous experiences on how to move forward. I will never stop living in my passion for healing and helping others and the way that I am able to stay in this work is by practicing what I preach. I feel that my gift is illuminating for others what is right in front of them so that their gifts can be shared and given to the world. I am in this work every day, and the more I commit to it, the more alive I feel and become."

Conclusion

Lisa Ingle-Stevens' narrative beautifully illustrates how dedication to personal growth and passion for empowering others can weave together to form a deeply impactful life and pilgrimage. Her journey from her first poignant yoga class to becoming a leader and mentor in the wellness community brings to light her commitment to promoting environments where individuals can thrive both personally and professionally. Through her work at The Union and The U Institute, Lisa continues to inspire a lifestyle of mindfulness, resilience, and continuous learning. Her story not only motivates you to pursue your callings with heart and vigor but also reminds you of the far-reaching impact you can have on your communities when you lead with passion and purpose.

Let us now examine another powerful case study from the late father of the authors of this book.

Don Alejandro: The Life of a Good Vibe Gangsta

The narrative of Mario Alejandro, affectionately known as Alex, is a sagacious illustration of the present chapter. From the lush landscapes of his native Guatemala in Central America to the charismatic communities of Texas, Alex's life journey was defined by his undying passion and commitment to whatever he pursued.

Starting on the coffee estate in Guatemala, Alex learned to administrate the delicate art of coffee cultivation under the guidance of his father, Carlos Enrique. He was not just involved in the process but mastered and administrated every detail from seed to roast. Known for his exceptional people skills, Alex became a beloved administrative figure among the coffee estate workers, handling everyone with respect and sincerity, strengthening a community of mutual trust and appreciation.

His life took a significant turn when he met his future wife, Rossi, a native Texan involved in international community development in Latin America. Their shared values and dreams led them to marry in Guatemala and eventually move to Texas amid growing safety concerns in Latin America due to civil unrest. In Texas, Alex's passions evolved as he embraced the role of a family man. He engaged in various entrepreneurial ventures, from service-based companies to real estate investments, always focusing on contributing positively to his family.

In addition to his entrepreneurial spirit and dedication to his family, Alex was sincerely committed to making a positive impact in his communities, both in Texas and Guatemala. His involvement ascended simple charity; Alex was hands-on in addressing the infrastructure needs of rural populations. Whether it was helping to install water purification systems to ensure clean drinking water, installing indoor and outdoor cooking stoves, or assisting in the development of other essential infrastructure, Alex was driven by a deep-seated belief in improving the quality of life for those less fortunate.

His efforts transcended borders and social classes, reflecting his understanding that real change comes from tangible, grassroots actions that address basic needs. Alex's dedication to these initiatives showcased his belief in a connected world where everyone deserves access to basic amenities, regardless of their geographical or social standing. This aspect of his life not only enriched the communities he touched but also set a profound example of cross-cultural solidarity and the impact one individual can have on the global stage.

His role as a grandfather to María Alejandra marked the peak of his passion. Alex's love and dedication to his granddaughter encapsulated his life's joys and achievements, instilling in her the same fervor for life and compassion for others that he possessed.

Here are some of Alex's stellar insights that will inspire you to pursue your own passions:

1. Adaptability: Embrace change and adapt your passions to new circumstances and opportunities, as Alex did when he moved from Guatemala to Texas.
2. Respect and Connect: Approach everyone with respect and take the time to genuinely connect with people, as these relationships can define and enrich your personal and professional life.
3. Commitment to Community: Engage actively in your community; giving back is not only fulfilling but also builds a network of support and shared goals.
4. Family First: Prioritize family in your pursuits; being a supportive partner and parent is a legacy that continues through generations.
5. Lifelong Learning: Always be open to learning new things, whether it is the intricacies of coffee roasting or the nuances of real estate.
6. Undertake Entrepreneurship: Do not be afraid to start new ventures. Entrepreneurship can be a rewarding way to express passion and create an impact.

7. Holistic Development: Invest in all aspects of your life, from vocation to personal growth to spiritual fulfillment to the appreciation of the natural world.
8. Find Joy in Small Moments: Like Alex's relationship with María Alejandra, sometimes the smallest moments carry the deepest meaning.
9. Resilience in Adversity: Face and accept challenges with courage and resilience, just as Alex did in dealing with his Parkinson's and dementia, along with other changes throughout his life.
10. Live Passionately: Put your heart into everything you do. Passion is the fuel that drives both success and satisfaction.

Through these lessons, Alex's life story not only serves as a guide for pursuing passions across different facets of life but also inspires others to lead a life filled with purpose, love, and the relentless pursuit of what truly matters. In reflecting on the life of Alex, it is clear that he not only pursued his passions but lived the ethos of a Good Vibe Gangsta. His journey from administering the coffee estate in Guatemala to the entrepreneurial ventures in Texas showcases a life lived with intention, warmth, and a steadfast commitment to positivity.

Alex's ability to cultivate respect and genuine connections with everyone he met, from his employees at the coffee estate to his neighbors in Texas, highlights his role as a natural Good Vibe Gangsta. He understood the constructive impact of considering people with kindness and dignity, creating an atmosphere where everyone felt valued and appreciated. This approach not only made him a beloved figure but also amplified the good vibes in his surroundings, making his communities better places to live.

His entrepreneurial spirit and dedication to community involvement further exemplified how a Good Vibe Gangsta channels their passions into actions that benefit others. Alex's ventures were not just businesses; they were opportunities to create jobs, solve problems, and contribute to the community's welfare. His commitment to charitable giving, even when managing his own challenges, emphasized his belief in the power of generosity and support.

As a family man, Alex's greatest legacy may be the love and lessons he imparted to his sons, Jimmy and Joey, and his cherished granddaughter, María Alejandra. His role as a grandfather was imbued with the joy and enthusiasm characteristic of a Good Vibe Gangsta, focusing on the positive and embracing every moment with love and laughter.

Alex's story concludes with a powerful reminder of the impact one individual can have by living passionately and positively. Through his life, Alex demonstrated that being a Good Vibe Gangsta is about much more than personal success; it is about inspiring, uplifting, and transforming the lives of others through genuine connections, community service, and a boundless zest for life. His legacy is a testament to the extensive effects of spreading good vibes, showing that the true measure of our lives lies in the joy and positivity we share with the world.

Conclusion

Now that you have explored the depths of finding and following your calling, you possess the knowledge and abilities necessary to seek out and pursue your true passion. This chapter has shown you the way, but it has also drawn attention to the roadblocks that may prevent you from reaching your goals, both personal and professional. As we move into the next chapter, where learning to accept failure will emerge as a cornerstone of building resilience and attaining long-term success, maintain this clarity and determination.

CHAPTER 2 SUMMARY

PURSUE PASSIONS

This chapter encourages you to identify and pursue your true passions to lead a fulfilling and impactful life.

DIAGNOSIS

Many people feel disconnected from their work and daily activities, lacking passion and motivation.

PROGNOSIS

Reflect on what brings you joy and satisfaction, and gradually align your life and career with these passions.

TREATMENT

Begin by exploring interests that resonate with you and plan small, actionable steps to integrate these passions into your life.

REQUIREMENTS

Determination to pursue what you love despite obstacles and societal expectations.

NEXT CHAPTER
Accept Failure

goodvibegangsta.com

CHAPTER 3
Accept Failure

Introduction

The word 'failure' carries many negative connotations and is frequently associated with fear and disappointment. However, failure is not only a possibility but also an inevitable and, more importantly, necessary part of the journey towards personal and professional growth. Accepting and growing from failure is not just a skill; it is a necessity for developing resilience, encouraging creativity, and laying the groundwork for success.

We will experience challenges and disappointments as we work toward our objectives, particularly those closely related to our personal callings. Although these moments of failure might be demoralizing, they also offer priceless opportunities for development and self-discovery. We can accept failures with openness and readiness to adapt if we shift our viewpoint from seeing them as bad outcomes to seeing them as necessary phases in the learning process.

Understanding Failure

In the realm of trial and error, where creativity and taking chances are primal components, failure is a common result. It is the inevitable counterpart of success; the two are inextricably linked. Every setback yields valuable lessons that, with careful consideration and analysis, can improve judgment, sharpen tactics, and provide one with a clearer grasp of their own strengths and weaknesses.

The Stigma of Failure

Failure is frequently stigmatized by society, linking it to a lack of competence or effort. This perception may give rise to a fear of taking risks or pushing boundaries. But to fully develop and realize our potential, we need to debunk these myths and adopt a more positive perspective on failure, one that promotes growth and learning from mistakes.

A New Perspective on Failure

This chapter seeks to redefine failure, turning it from an enemy to be dreaded to an ally to be revered. We will look at how embracing failure as a necessary part of success can help eliminate the stigma and anxiety around it and promote a more daring and resilient way of living and working. We will discover how to develop emotional and psychological resilience, process and learn from setbacks, and use the lessons learned to drive progress.

Navigating This Chapter

We will uncover the hidden worth in setbacks and learn how to use them as fuel for future success as we progress through this chapter. The lessons in this section are intended to assist you in developing a resilient attitude that not only endures the difficulties of following a vocation but flourishes because of them. This introduction to accepting and learning from failure aims to equip you with the tools to turn every setback into a springboard for a successful comeback through firsthand accounts, psychological research, and helpful guidance.

Accepting the lessons from our mistakes helps us grow not only on our own journeys but also on the paths of those around us. We set an example and promote an ambiance where learning is valued more highly than success. This shift in perspective can have a significant impact on how we define success and address obstacles, laying the groundwork for a meaningful and influential life.

The Inevitability of Failure

Understanding the Certainty of Setbacks

Failure is not only a possibility in any undertaking requiring expansion, creativity, or change—it is inevitable. Anyone who wants to push limits and accomplish big goals must acknowledge this fundamental fact. It is imperative to realize that, regardless of how great a company may seem on the outside, failure affects every individual and organization.

Why Failure is Inevitable

1. Task Complexity: Unexpected difficulties and roadblocks are more likely to arise when tasks and projects become more ambitious and complicated. This complexity frequently corresponds to an increased likelihood of failure, particularly when branching out or innovating.
2. Limits of Knowledge and Experience: Regardless of our degree of expertise or knowledge, there are certain things we can never know or experience. These limitations may cause mistakes in decision-making or execution, which could lead to failure.
3. Unpredictable Settings: Whether they are work-related, personal, or social, our settings are variable and frequently unpredictable. Failures can result from techniques that were previously successful becoming ineffective due to changes in technology, market conditions, or social trends.

The Role of Risk-Taking in Failure

While taking chances raises the possibility of failure, it is also necessary for achieving extraordinary accomplishments. Leaders, innovators, and pioneers recognize that to achieve meaningful progress, they must take risks and go into uncharted territory with unclear results. Taking risks may lead to both significant failures and spectacular successes, so it is a double-edged sword.

Normalizing Failure in the Pursuit of Success

To accept failure as inevitable, it is crucial to normalize it in relation to success and progress. We may change the way we go about achieving our objectives by realizing that every setback is a learning opportunity rather than a barrier. By normalizing failure, we:

- Reduce the Stigma: Lowering the psychological barriers and the stigma around failing makes it easier to take necessary risks.
- Foster Learning Habits: Create an environment where every failure is seen as a chance for growth and positive change.
- Build Resilience: Enhancing our capacity to overcome obstacles helps us become more resilient and tenacious overall.

Failure as Part of the Learning Curve

Every successful individual or business has had setbacks in the past. These setbacks frequently constitute fundamental elements of their learning curves, offering insights and lessons that propel subsequent achievement. It is critical to accept failure as a necessary part of this learning process. It involves realizing that every obstacle we face imparts knowledge about our tactics, choices, or actions that we may apply to improve our future plans.

Conclusion

Accepting that failure is inevitable does not mean giving up on oneself; rather, it means preparing to take on challenges head-on and equipping oneself with the knowledge that every setback is a necessary component of the path to success. This section lays the foundation for creating effective failure management strategies, ensuring that failures, when they happen, help us grow and achieve our goals in the long run.

Reframing Failure

Introduction to Reframing Failure

Reframing failure involves shifting our perspective to view failures as invaluable learning opportunities rather than as disastrous outcomes. This cognitive reorganization changes our perception of and response to failure, enabling us to remain resilient and motivated in the face of adversity. It is about viewing failure not as a sign of defeat and loss, but as an opportunity for development and progress.

The Power of Positive Reframing

Positive reframing involves acknowledging the disappointment of failure while simultaneously emphasizing the valuable feedback and lessons it offers. It does not imply ignoring the negatives aspects of failure. This method maintains motivation and self-worth while cultivating a problem-solving mindset that is primal for ongoing progress.

Strategies for Reframing Failure

1. Recognize and Address Negative Thoughts: It is normal to lapse into negative thought patterns when confronted with failure. Recognize these thoughts and challenge them. Substitute them with more rational ideas that consider the lessons discovered and the possibility of future achievement.
2. Emphasize Effort and Growth: Prioritize the effort invested in the task and the learning that results from the experience rather than concentrating only on the final product. This shift in perspective can aid the development of a resilient mindset, in which the learning process itself is valuable.
3. Establish Learning Objectives: Set learning objectives that emphasize the acquisition of information and skills, independent of the project's success or failure, and in addition to outcome objectives. This guarantees that each encounter is worthwhile and advances both one's pursuits and personal development.

Creating Learning Customs

Creating a learning culture within oneself or an organization is helpful in reframing failure in a productive way. Curiosity, constant progress, and valuing the process over the pursuit of results are all celebrated in this mind set.

1. Promote Open Communication: Establish environments where people feel comfortable talking about their mistakes and the lessons they have learned from them.

This transparency enriches the group's overall knowledge and experience while also normalizing failure.
2. Normalize Failures Through Storytelling: Share stories of well-known triumphs that were preceded by significant failures. By exposing these tales, we can normalize failures and emphasize how important they were in producing important discoveries.
3. Feedback Loops: Establish regular feedback loops to help identify what worked, what did not, and what needs to be changed. This constructive feedback promotes a more nuanced understanding of failure.

Long-Term Benefits of Reframing Failure

Reframing failure provides several long-term benefits that are critical for sustainable success:

1. Improved Problem-Solving: People get better at solving problems by learning from their mistakes. They become more skilled at spotting possible problems and coming up with workable answers.
2. More Invention: People are more willing to take clever risks and exhibit greater creativity and invention in an atmosphere that views failure as a teaching tool rather than a setback.
3. Greater Resilience: Those who redefine failure exhibit greater resilience. They are more inclined to persevere in the face of difficulties and are less prone to be deterred by setbacks.

Conclusion

Anyone hoping to succeed in complex, unpredictable circumstances where setbacks are inevitable must learn to reframe failure. By altering the way we view failure, we can harness its potential to propel our growth, resilience, and success. This reframing not only aids individuals in better navigating their personal trajectories but also strengthens, adapts, and innovates the culture of any organization or community to which they belong.

Strategies for Handling Failure

Introduction to Handling Failure

For anyone aspiring to great success, learning how to deal with failure is crucial. It requires not just flexibility and resilience but also practical strategies that turn setbacks into advancements. This section provides practical strategies for handling setbacks and learning from them to make sure they enable both professional and personal development.

Building Emotional Resilience

1. Practice Mindfulness: Engage in mindfulness activities to maintain perspective and composure when faced with obstacles. Practicing mindfulness can help better manage stress and prevent strong emotions from impairing judgement.
2. Seek Support: In challenging times, lean on your network of friends, family, and coworkers for assistance. Sharing

your experiences and feelings can lessen emotional burdens and provide fresh perspectives for support.
3. Develop Healthy Coping Mechanisms: Replace negative coping strategies (like denial or avoidance) with constructive ones (like journaling, exercise, or artistic endeavors) that can aid in the healthy processing of emotions.

Analyzing Failures to Extract Lessons

1. Conduct a Post-Analysis: Spend some time methodically reviewing what went wrong after a failure. Identify the choices and procedures that produced the result. What was effective? What did not work? How could something be done better the next time?
2. Record Insights: Keep a failure log or notebook where you jot down specifics of every setback, along with your analyses of what went wrong and the lessons you learned. This documentation can prove to be an invaluable asset for future projects.
3. Modify Strategies in Light of Learnings: Apply the knowledge you have gleamed from your analysis to improve your strategy. This could involve changing your strategies, adjusting your schedule, or even reevaluating your objectives to ensure they remain relevant and achievable.

Incorporating Lessons into Future Plans

1. Make Modest Adjustments: Rather than completely changing your strategy all at once, incorporate the

lessons you have learned into your plans by making small, achievable adjustments. This makes it possible to continuously tweak and improve.
2. Implement Early Warning Signals: Using data from past mistakes, create indicators that warn you as soon as something starts to go off course. These can help you change direction before small problems become significant setbacks.
3. Utilize Scenario Planning: Participate in scenario planning regularly to foresee possible problems and provide solutions for them. By being proactive, you can mitigate the effects of future mistakes.

Upholding a Milieu of Learning

1. Encourage a Learning-Oriented Environment: Foster a mindset that values ongoing learning and development, whether in a group context or individually. To increase understanding and promote creativity, encourage questioning and curiosity.
2. Praise Effort and Learning Rather Than Just Success: Shift the emphasis from results to effort and learning. Regardless of whether they are successful right away, promptly acknowledge and applaud attempts to implement novel tactics or concepts.
3. Share Failures and Learnings: Cultivate the habit of sharing your mistakes and the knowledge you have gained with others. This can help create a community where learning from one another is valued and failure is normalized.

Conclusion

Effectively managing setbacks involves not only bouncing back but also bouncing forward. You can ensure that every setback becomes a driving force for development and progress by cultivating a culture of learning, strengthening emotional resilience, closely examining mistakes, and applying lessons learned to future plans. These techniques help spark a mindset where learning and continual development are accepted as the standard, as well as preparing you to deal with obstacles in the future more skillfully. This strategy not only aids in professional and personal growth, but it also makes it easier to attain long-term success in a way that is both gratifying and sustainable.

Creating a Supportive Environment

Introduction to a Supportive Environment

Effectively managing failure and turning it into a learning opportunity requires a supportive environment. In addition to offering emotional safety, such a setting promotes open dialogue, collaborative learning, and creativity. In this section, we look at how individuals, groups, and institutions can create settings that accept failure as a necessary part of growth and development, rather than just tolerating it.

Characteristics of a Supportive Environment

A truly supportive environment includes several constitutive characteristics:

1. Psychological Safety: People do not feel afraid to share their opinions, pose questions, own up to their mistakes,

or express concerns out of fear of rejection or retaliation. This safety is fundamental to creating an environment where it is acceptable to learn from mistakes.
2. Honest and Open Communication: Promoting open and honest communication makes failure less stigmatized and makes it easier for people to share ideas and solutions. This transparency makes sure that lessons are shared broadly and that mistakes are productively discussed.
3. Mutual Respect: Regardless of results, mutual respect among peers and between staff and leadership ensures that every member feels appreciated. Maintaining motivation and involvement, particularly following disappointments, requires this kind of respect.

Strategies for Building a Supportive Environment

1. Leadership by Example: Leaders should set an example for the behaviors they want to see in others by how they respond to their own mistakes. Leaders who are willing to share their failures and the lessons they have learned can set a good example for others to follow.
2. Structured Debriefings: Regardless of the project's or important decision's outcome, hold regular debriefing sessions afterward. These discussions should focus on the lessons learned and how they may be applied moving forward.
3. Recognition and Rewards: Provide mechanisms for acknowledgment and rewards that place an emphasis on creative endeavors and learning objectives rather than just accomplishments. Awards for the 'Best Learned

Lesson' or recognition for groups that bravely take on difficult tasks might fall under this category.

Promoting Risk-Taking

To encourage an environment that supports failure:

1. Evaluated Risk-Taking: Promote evaluated risk-taking by outlining precise standards for what qualifies as a reasonable risk. Provide guidance and encouragement so that individuals and groups can determine when and how to take risks.
2. Resource Allocation: Allocate funds and time specifically for trial projects whose results are unpredictable. This demonstrates organizational dedication to learning and innovation even in situations when success is not assured.
3. Safety Nets: Provide safety nets to assist individuals and groups in bouncing back from setbacks. These could include access to project rescue teams, mentors, or buffer resources to help deal with the fallout from failed endeavors.

Sharing and Learning from Failures

Creating channels for sharing failures and their lessons is vital:

1. Knowledge Sharing Platforms: Share success and failure stories via newsletters, intranets, or regular meetings. Emphasizing these experiences helps encourage a culture of learning and normalize failure.

2. Learning Workshops: Arrange workshops where teams can showcase their unplanned projects, discuss the lessons they learned, and brainstorm ideas for how these lessons can apply to other projects in the future.
3. Cross-Team Sessions: Organize get-togethers for various teams to exchange knowledge and perspectives. This idea exchange can result in more innovative and improved methods overall.

Conclusion

To succeed in a complicated and competitive world, it is imperative for individuals or organizations to establish a supporting atmosphere. You can boost resilience, spur innovation, and guarantee ongoing development by cultivating a climate that sees failure as a learning opportunity, encourages risk-taking, and promotes open communication and mutual respect. This supportive environment is crucial for overcoming failures as well as utilizing them as engines for development and achievement.

Long-Term Benefits of Embracing Failure

Introduction to the Benefits of Failure

Even while facing failure head-on might be difficult, accepting it and growing from it can have significant long-term benefits. A positive outlook on failure can not only increase personal adaptation and resilience but also advance organizational and professional development. This section examines the long-term benefits of handling failure well and growing from it.

Boosted Problem-Solving Skills

The improvement of problem-solving abilities is one of the biggest benefits of accepting failure. Every failure presents its own set of obstacles to overcome, and doing so sharpens your skills to evaluate, plan, and perform better in similar circumstances in the future.

1. Critical Thinking: Regularly examining mistakes helps you develop your critical thinking abilities by breaking down complicated circumstances to figure out what went wrong.
2. Creative Solutions: Developing creative problem-solving skills through learning from failure frequently requires thinking outside the box.

Increased Innovation

Individuals and organizations that accept failure tend to be more creative. Allowing oneself to fail lowers barriers to trying out novel concepts and may result in groundbreaking progress.

1. Risk-Taking: Taking evaluated risks is encouraged when failures are accepted as a necessary part of the learning process. This is achieved by accepting failure.
2. Iterative Development: Companies who want to create better products might take a more iterative approach, learning from each failure encountered during testing phases.

Stronger Resilience

Effectively dealing with failures builds resilience, which is essential for long-term success in any endeavor.

1. Emotional Stability: Acquiring the skill to manage the emotional fallout from failure helps maintain emotional stability.
2. Persistence: Facing challenges and overcoming setbacks cultivates a spirit of perseverance that is mandatory for taking on challenging tasks and long-term objectives.

Improved Adaptability

Failure is a great teacher of adaptability because it makes you reevaluate your goals and tactics and prepares you to adjust, as necessary.

1. Learning Agility: Individuals acquire the ability to swiftly absorb failure-related lessons and adapt to new circumstances.
2. Environmental Sensitivity: Increase environmental awareness equips organizations to better foresee and address emerging issues.

Deeper Knowledge and Expertise

Each failure is a learning opportunity that contributes to deeper knowledge and expertise in your field.

1. Expert Insight: Failures frequently yield deeper understandings of processes, consumer needs, and market insights than successes do.

2. Professional Development: Professional development and recognition are often advanced by the experience gained from conquering obstacles and setbacks.

Cultural Transformation

A team's or organization's culture can be completely changed to become more lively, open, and productive, by adapting a positive approach to failure.

1. Collaborative Learning: Communities that accept failure are typically more cooperative because exchanging insights on setbacks helps individuals learn from past mistakes and promote teamwork.
2. Trust and Openness: When failure is destigmatized, team members feel more comfortable voicing concerns and owning up to mistakes, which creates greater trust and openness.

Conclusion

We have discussed the transformational potential of accepting our mistakes and setbacks as necessary parts of our personal development. This section illustrates that failure is a valuable teacher that helps you become more resilient and wiser, rather than a reflection of your ability. By reinterpreting failure as a learning opportunity rather than a roadblock, you can unlock greater potential for advancement and creativity. As you move forward, do not forget that every setback adds value to your experience and gives you the strength and knowledge you need to proceed with courage and uniqueness. Allow this fresh perspective to encourage you to take on obstacles head-on, knowing that every experience makes you a completer and more accomplished version of yourself.

Real-Life Examples of 'Accept Failure'

In this section, we dive into the transformational potential of accepting failures by telling the tales of people who personify the Good Vibe Gangsta. Each story not only demonstrates how the principles covered in this book may be put into practice but also showcases the stunning results that can occur when someone dares to step beyond the conventional.

Rubén Cantú: Bridging Worlds and Embracing Resilience

Rubén's story is a powerful narrative of overcoming adversity, pioneering change, and embodying the Good Vibe Gangsta spirit through dedicated social entrepreneurship and community service. His journey is marked not just by his achievements but also by his relentless commitment to promoting peace, understanding, and love across diverse communities.

His life began with his family's immigration from Mexico, bringing with them a rich collage of Indigenous, European, African, and Asian heritage. This multicultural background laid the foundation for what Rubén would later understand as his mission: to act as a bridge for building global peace and communal healing through love and understanding. His journey through life has been a demonstration of the belief that humanity grows stronger each time someone walks by faith, trusts in their well-being, and shares that trust with others.

Starting his first radio show at fourteen and founding his first company at sixteen, Rubén's early ventures into the world of media and entrepreneurship set the stage for his later accomplishments. These formative experiences were not without challenges. Each failure taught Rubén valuable lessons about resilience, the power of community, and the importance of maintaining integrity in every endeavor.

As a first-generation college student from a family of migrant workers, Rubén was both a pioneer and a bearer of responsibility. His academic journey took him to the University of Texas at Austin, where he was one of the first Mexican American students to complete his master's program—a role he assumed with honor and a sense of duty. He was also the very first student from his High School to attend UT Austin. The challenges and setbacks he faced along the way did not deter him but instead deepened his commitment to creating a better world for his family and community.

In 2009, Rubén launched CORE Media Enterprises, evolving it from a full-scale video production company into a marketing strategy agency. His leadership here emphasized creating content that shifts consciousness toward intentional, responsible, and loving interactions with one another and the environment. His work with CORE Media was a precursor to his later ventures, including founding Austin's first social impact accelerator and fund and spearheading innovative educational programs such as the Startup Superstars for Title 1 public schools and the LevelUp Institute for college students.

Rubén's passion for social entrepreneurship led him to help found a global community with the United Nations Foundation in 2013. +Social Good connected local activists who use technology to create grassroots initiatives, helping shape global conversations on sustainable development goals. His pioneering efforts also brought the first-ever conference for social impact to SXSW in 2013, demonstrating his ability to use platforms for significant social impact.

Rubén's dedication to his community and social impact has not gone unnoticed. He has received numerous recognitions, including the 'Austin Under 40 for Youth and Education' and has been nominated multiple times for 'Changemaker of the Year.' His work continues to inspire and motivate, focusing on breaking barriers and valuing peace and prosperity both locally and internationally.

Rubén's journey exemplifies the essence of learning from failure—a core principle of the Good Vibe Gangsta philosophy. His life's work shows how resilience, combined with a commitment to social good and community building, can transform personal challenges into opportunities for widespread positive change. In this book, Rubén's story serves as a light of hope and a practical example for all who strive to make a meaningful impact in the world while navigating their paths of personal and professional growth.

Here are the comments Rubén made during our Q&A session regarding the book, which we were honored to host.

Q1: What role does failure play in your personal and professional life, and how have you learned to accept it?

A1: "In a world that idolizes perfection and wunderkinds who always get it right, we often miss the full narrative—the trials and missteps that lead to success. Our society glorifies the end results and overlooks the journey, including the failures that teach us necessary lessons.

In my experience, failure is not just an obstacle; it is an integral part of the path to success. It is a snapshot in time, a moment that might seem unfortunate but is a setup for the next opportunity. Take, for instance, when I launched a high school entrepreneurship program. It succeeded initially and even made it to SXSW. However, it faced funding challenges that halted its expansion. This apparent setback forced me to analyze other avenues, shifting from high school to college programs, subsequently leading to greater impacts and successes.

I have learned to see every failure as an event happening for me, not to me. This shift in perspective has turned setbacks into setups, paving the way for future successes. By taking in failure as part of the journey, I have maneuvered through challenges and turned them into opportunities, continuously moving toward larger goals."

Q2: How has mindfulness influenced your perception of and reaction to failure?

A2: "Mindfulness has fundamentally changed how I perceive and react to failure by grounding me in the present. It shifts my focus from relentlessly pursuing goals to appreciating the journey, emphasizing *being* over *having*. This perspective allows me to live more fully in the moment, where clarity looms and false narratives dissolve.

In practice, mindfulness helps me discern the truths from the stories I tell myself. A method taught to me by my mentor and friend, Ruth Glendinning, involves asking four critical questions when faced with potential stressors: Is this true? Has this been true? Could this be true? Should this be true? This framework helps navigate the reality of situations, grounding responses in the present rather than past fears or future anxieties.

This approach shifts the control from external circumstances to internal choices. It encourages asking whether actions are driven by fear or by a commitment to the life I aim to create. Each decision, each word, shapes our reality—choosing fear breeds more fear, while choosing love cultivates a positive future.

Conclusively, mindfulness offers a tool to transform how we handle failure—not as an endpoint but as a critical, enlightening part of our personal and professional growth narratives. It is about choosing liberation through love over the constraints of fear every single moment."

Q3: Can you share a specific instance where you faced significant failure, and how did being mindful help, you cope and learn from that experience?

A3: "Reflecting on my experiences, I realize I do not dwell on failures; instead, I transform them into lessons almost instantly. However, a notable period of challenge was during my tenure at Apple from 2005 to 2008. Initially, I was thriving, involved in high-profile projects like the launch of the iPhone, and recognized repeatedly as an employee of the month.

As time progressed, though, my enthusiasm waned. My performance metrics plummeted, and without supportive management, I felt stalled and overlooked. The effusive drive with which I began had dimmed to the point where, during a break, I decided I could not return to my desk. I resigned, communicating my decision to my supervisor via a message.

This low point coincided with my acceptance into graduate school. Surprisingly, Apple not only respected my decision to leave but also provided a severance package that supported me financially as I transitioned into academia. This period of failure at Apple, painful as it was, nudged me toward a path better in tune with my values and aspirations.

Mindfulness played a significant role in this transition. It taught me the importance of being present and recognizing when a situation no longer serves my growth. It also stressed the need for self-advocacy and seeking mentorship, which I had previously shied away from due to fear and mistrust.

Essentially, what seemed like a setback was a redirection towards entrepreneurship—a path that has allowed me to establish and lead my own companies. This experience taught me that failures, however disheartening, are often setups for greater achievements. It was this mindful approach that allowed me to convert what felt like a professional low into a launchpad for my true aspirations."

Q4: What advice would you give to someone who fears failure or struggles to overcome a past failure?

A4: "Fear of failure is basically fear of an illusion. This fear arises from how we interpret events, much like a child learning to walk. Despite the inevitable falls, each child continues trying, undeterred by the fear of falling again. This analogy illustrates that fear of failure is merely a perspective, not an absolute.

Many of us find ourselves trapped by past narratives that have not been fully processed, leaving us in a protective state against potential pain. This state may feel safe because it is familiar, but it is not free. Recognizing this is the first step to overcoming the fear of failure. True growth demands that we release these stories and allow intentional progress to guide us. Change is inevitable, but progress is a choice that requires deliberate action.

If you are hesitant to move forward, understand that this hesitation is tied to unprocessed narratives within your nervous system. Championing growth means allowing past pains to be processed and inviting love to lead you forward. Every setback is part of the journey and is inherently temporary.

To truly live, we must not allow ourselves to be defined by specific events but by the ongoing narrative we choose to sign off on. Define yourself by your values and the narratives you actively create, not by the incidents of your past. This mindset allows you to cherish the present and move forward with a sense of purpose and freedom."

Q5: How do you plan to use your experiences with failure to influence your future goals or projects?

A5: "Each experience with failure sets me up for the next lesson I need to learn. Knowing life is a continuous journey allows me to not fixate on outcomes but to enjoy the process, embracing that this too will pass.

Every time I faced failure, I moved forward; I never stayed stagnant. There were moments of reflection, sometimes days or weeks, where I dwelled on what could have been. But each time, I released those thoughts, learned from the experience, and stepped into the unknown. This is when new chapters unfolded.

I have come to recognize that I am both my greatest obstacle and my greatest liberator. The power to grow and overcome setbacks lies in my choices. I have learned to not just win but to truly live by accepting humility and the willingness to surrender to the process.

Life is not just about success; it is meant to be experienced in its entirety, including failures. Embracing this full spectrum ensures a richer, more complete life. Instead of fearing potential failures, I look forward to what each experience will teach me. Nothing is fatal unless we allow our fears to hold us back. By choosing to view the world as a series of growth opportunities, I open myself up to a life of continuous learning and evolving, preparing me for whatever comes next."

Conclusion

Rubén Cantú's life exemplifies an exuberant dedication to promoting peace and understanding through resourceful community engagement and social entrepreneurship. His ability to apply personal experiences and professional expertise to bridge cultural divides and inspire collective action is confirmation of his deep commitment to societal improvement. Rubén's journey from humble beginnings to becoming an influencer in social impact serves as an inspiring model for anyone aiming to make a significant impact in their community. His continued efforts to promote sustainable development and his role in shaping global conversations around social good underscore a legacy of meaningful change and enduring impact.

Now let us look at a lovely fatherhood case study by one of this book's authors.

Joey & Jandra: The Father and Daughter Bond is Unbreakable

In the woven narrative of Joey's life, his chapter with María Alejandra's mother, though fraught with challenges, serves as a powerful catalyst for personal growth and reflection. Despite the relationship not unfolding as anticipated, Joey has maintained a steadfast commitment to positivity and goodwill for the best interest of his daughter. He consistently wishes the best for her mother, embodying a spirit of kindness and understanding. This approach not only helps maintain a peaceful coexistence but also advocates for a nurturing environment for María Alejandra.

With her bright smile and cheerful eyes, María Alejandra became Joey's guiding light, showing him the boundless possibilities of life when viewed through the lens of love and commitment. This transformation was not just about adapting to life's unexpected turns but about thriving in them and finding meaning in the connections that shape us. Joey's journey with his daughter has become an authentication to the power of perspective, demonstrating that out of complex situations can come the most fulfilling rewards.

Joey's relationship with his daughter illuminates the vital role a father plays in shaping a girl's perception of male figures. Through his actions, he teaches María Alejandra the standards by which she should expect to be respected by men. His respect, compassion, and unwavering support offer her a framework of how positive interactions should look. Joey is more than just a parent; he is a role model demonstrating the virtues of respect and kindness.

The respect that he shows toward her mother, despite their differences, are integral lessons for María Alejandra. They emphasize the importance of treating others with dignity, regardless of the circumstances. This backdrop of resilience and benevolence not only strengthens the bond between father and daughter but also sets a foundation for María Alejandra's future relationships, teaching her the intrinsic value of respect and empathy in all interactions.

Navigating a parallel parenting situation like the one that Joey faces can present unique challenges but also valuable lessons. Here are some of his valuable insights and strategies that might help you if you are ever in similar circumstances:

1. Focus on Your Child's Well-being: Prioritize your child's needs and emotional health above conflicts with the other

parent. Keep your child's best interests at heart, ensuring they feel loved and supported by both parents.
2. Maintain Clear Boundaries: In parallel parenting, it is especially important to establish and respect boundaries. This means having clear, structured arrangements about parenting time, responsibilities, and communication. Boundaries can help reduce conflicts and provide a stable environment for your child.
3. Effective Communication: Keep communication with the other parent business-like, respectful, and to the point, focusing solely on your child's needs. Tools like email or parenting apps can help keep interactions straightforward and documented.
4. Emotional Management: Managing your emotions is crucial. It is important to find healthy outlets for your feelings, such as talking to a therapist or counselor, which can prevent any negative impact on your child.
5. Consistency and Stability: Try to maintain consistency in parenting styles and routines between both households as much as possible. This helps create a sense of security and predictability for your child, which is essential for their development.
6. Legal and Practical Preparation: Understand your legal rights and responsibilities. If necessary, consult with a lawyer to ensure you are informed about your parental rights and any required legal steps.
7. Personal Growth and Support: Take care of your own mental and emotional health. Engage in activities that you enjoy and maintain a supportive network of friends

and family. Personal well-being is essential to being a good parent.
8. Modeling Respect and Maturity: Demonstrate how to handle disagreements and conflicts with respect and maturity. This is a powerful lesson for your child on how to manage difficult situations in their own life.
9. Stay Engaged in Your Child's Life: Be actively involved in your child's life. Attend school events, know their interests, and be present. Your involvement has a significant impact on their self-esteem and development.
10. Narcissism Is Real: Educate yourself as much as possible on the topic so that you can identify early signs across the spectrum. Then you can develop healthy strategies appropriately along the way, such as the 'gray rock' approach, among others.

By focusing on these areas, you can provide a supportive and loving environment for your child despite the complexities of a parallel parenting arrangement. Joey's journey through the complexities of a challenging relationship and his role as a father exemplify the essence of being a Good Vibe Gangsta. Amid adversity, he chooses to lead with positivity, understanding, and compassion—qualities that not only maintain harmony but also cultivate a nurturing environment for his daughter, María Alejandra.

His unwavering commitment to spreading good vibes, even in less-than-ideal circumstances, serves as a powerful model for others. Joey demonstrates that true strength lies in the ability to remain kind and hopeful, to wish well for others, and to function as a beacon of positivity. By doing so, he not only enriches his own life but also sets a formidable example for his daughter, teaching her to always stand her ground and the invaluable lesson of treating others with respect and kindness, regardless of the situation.

In closing, Joey's actions and attitudes reinforce the notion that being a Good Vibe Gangsta is not just about facing life with a smile but also about making a positive impact on those around you, particularly in the roles we play within our families. His story is a compelling call to all, emphasizing that by embodying these principles, one can navigate even the most challenging waters and emerge not just unscathed but enriched. It is a validation of the power of positivity and the profound influence it can have on the world, one interaction at a time.

Conclusion

In embracing your failures as hidden treasures, you have learned one of life's most valuable lessons. This chapter has equipped you with strategies to convert setbacks into setups for future successes. Let the resilience you have cultivated be your guide as you move to the next chapter, where the spirit of 'Afford To Care' will challenge you to extend your positive impact beyond the scope of personal achievement to community and global betterment.

The Flores Brothers

CHAPTER 3 SUMMARY

ACCEPT FAILURE

This chapter discusses the importance of viewing failures as opportunities for growth and learning.

DIAGNOSIS

Fear of failure prevents many from taking risks and hampers personal and professional development.

PROGNOSIS

Shift your perspective to see failure as a necessary step towards success and a source of invaluable insights.

TREATMENT

Reflect on past failures to extract lessons and apply these learnings to future challenges.

REQUIREMENTS

A mindset shift towards resilience and the courage to face and embrace failures.

NEXT CHAPTER
Afford To Care

goodvibegangsta.com

CHAPTER 4

Afford To Care

Introduction

The idea of setting aside time to genuinely care for others—in both personal and professional domains—can sometimes feel like a luxury in today's hectic and fiercely competitive world. The 'Afford To Care' ideology, however, refutes this notion, claiming that compassion and community service are necessary elements of both a successful career and a fulfilling life, not merely optional extras. This chapter examines the importance of caring, its benefits for both us and those around us, and practical strategies for incorporating caring values into various facets of our lives.

Why 'Afford To Care' Matters

The idea of 'Afford To Care' goes outward of simple benevolence. It includes a proactive strategy for developing connections, increasing emotional intelligence, and creating strong, supportive communities. It translates to leadership philosophies that value understanding and empathy in the workplace, which can promote better teamwork and increased employee satisfaction. In the intimate sphere, it strengthens ties and deepens connections, adding significance to life.

Caring in a Self-Centric World

The world in which we live frequently places a premium on personal success and accomplishment. In an environment like this, it may seem paradoxical to show others care—to take the time to comprehend their struggles, support their wellbeing, and assist in patronizing their success. But according to 'Afford To Care,' taking care of others is a smart way to live and work that may have a big impact on the world, improve one's own wellbeing, and strengthen professional ties, among other benefits.

The Dual Benefits of Caring

Giving and receiving are both enriched when someone cares for another. Giving of oneself produces good feelings connected with helping others, which can lead to improved happiness, satisfaction, and even health advantages for the giver. The advantages are clear and substantial for those who receive them: being supported and shown compassion can result in improved mental and physical health, increased cooperation and trust, and a higher likelihood of overcoming obstacles.

Navigating This Chapter

This chapter will examine several aspects related to properly being able to 'Afford To Care'. We will cover the importance of instilling compassion in business practices and leadership, balancing personal and professional obligations with caring, and the impact of community involvement on societal wellbeing. There will be helpful tips on how to incorporate care into your daily routine in a way that is sustainable, enriching rather than draining, and consistent with your larger life objectives.

Conclusion

You will have a better knowledge of how caring can be incorporated into your life in a seamless manner by the end of this chapter, which will change the way you interact with people and perceive your place in society. 'Afford To Care' is a practical guide to leading a prosperous and deeply fulfilling life that leaves a legacy of positive influence: it is more than just a philosophy.

Understanding 'Afford To Care'

Introduction to 'Afford To Care'

Although there are many ways to interpret the phrase 'Afford To Care,' at its foundation, it denotes a dedication to incorporating kindness and volunteerism into all facets of one's life. To grasp this idea, one must acknowledge that showing compassion is both a moral duty and a practical strategy that can enhance personal fulfillment and professional success.

Core Elements of 'Afford To Care'

1. Compassion as a Daily Practice: 'Afford To Care' emphasizes the importance of practicing compassion regularly, not just during difficult circumstances or when it is convenient. This involves paying attention to what

others are saying, empathizing with their pain, and offering a helping hand without expecting anything in return.
2. Community Involvement: 'Afford To Care' encourages proactive participation in community projects as well as individual acts of kindness. This can involve organizing or participating in volunteer work, contributing to local causes, or engaging in civic endeavors that enhance the welfare of all.
3. Sustainable Caring: To genuinely 'Afford To Care,' one must offer care in a sustainable way. This means providing care in a balanced manner that prevents burnout. It entails establishing limits, placing self-care first, and striking a balance so that you can take care of other people without sacrificing your own needs.

The Importance of Caring Today

Caring is a powerful counterforce that promotes understanding and connection in a society that can sometimes appear divided and uncaring. Here's why compassion is so vital in today's world:

1. Social Cohesion: By nurturing connections between diverse populations, caring strengthens the social fabric. It encourages tolerance and empathy, qualities that are vital in a multicultural and globalized world.
2. Personal Well-Being: Research indicates that people who volunteer and perform acts of kindness lead happier and more fulfilled lives. The sense of fulfillment and purpose derived from personal accomplishments is often enhanced by caring.

3. Professional Benefits: Caring animates a more happy and cooperative work atmosphere. Leaders who genuinely care about the welfare of their staff members tend to inspire greater degrees of dedication, loyalty, and output.

Practical Applications of 'Afford To Care'

Incorporating 'Afford To Care' into daily life requires intentional actions:

1. In Personal Relationships: Show that you care about your friends' and family's lives and struggles by checking in with them on a regular basis, lending a helping hand when needed, and being present during conversations.
2. At Work: Put in place procedures that promote staff members' well-being, facilitate candid communication, and honor initiatives that uplift the workplace aura.
3. In the Community: Give your time and expertise to neighborhood organizations, take part in activities and planning, and support policies that help the less fortunate.

Challenges and Solutions

While the benefits of caring are significant, there are challenges:

1. Time Restraints: A lot of people believe they have too much on their plates to fit in caring activities. This can be handled by selecting volunteer endeavors that complement current obligations or by including tiny deeds of kindness into regular conversations.
2. Emotional Overload: Taking care of people all the time can be emotionally taxing. Setting limits and engaging in

self-care are of the essence for preserving your emotional and mental well-being.

Conclusion

Our interactions with the environment around us can be changed by comprehending and putting into practice 'Afford To Care.' It comes down to consciously choosing to invest in others' well-being, and consequently, our own. As we dig more into the practical applications of this idea, we will look at methods that people and groups can utilize to integrate compassion into their daily lives, safeguarding individual development and group cohesion.

The Importance of Compassion in Professional Life

Introduction to Compassion at Work

In the workplace, compassion transcends mere benevolence. It involves compassionate leadership, awareness of colleagues' needs on both personal and professional levels, and creating an atmosphere where people are respected and understood. Bringing compassion into the workplace increases organizational effectiveness and individual job satisfaction.

Building Strong Relationships Through Compassion

1. Open Communication and Trust: Compassion reinforces trust between management and staff. Communication among team members is more honest and open when leaders show sincere concern for their well-being both personally and professionally. Building cooperation, resolving disputes, and maintaining open lines of

communication within the company all depend on this trust.
2. Employee Loyalty and Retention: Employee loyalty and retention are stronger in compassionate organizations. Workers are more likely to stay with an organization where they are treated with respect and feel valued as people and employees. This stabilizes the workforce and maintains organizational knowledge by lowering turnover and the related costs of onboarding new hires.
3. Improved Team Collaboration: Teams with compassionate members have better interpersonal relationships. Team members are better able to collaborate and leverage individual strengths and weaknesses to improve overall productivity when they are aware of and empathetic to each other's challenges.

The Role of Compassionate Leadership

1. Setting an Example for Emotional Intelligence: Compassionate leaders often possess high emotional intelligence. They are skilled at identifying both their own and other's emotions and managing their responses accordingly. This skill is basic for successfully managing a team, particularly during stressful or transitional times.
2. Encouraging Workers: Leaders who demonstrate compassion have a great ability to inspire others. By appreciating individual contributions and approaching problems sympathetically, they motivate their staff. This approach often motivates better performance and increased productivity.

3. **Establishing a Supportive Work Environment:** Compassionate leaders manage a supportive work environment by prioritizing their workers' welfare first. In addition to meeting professional needs, this also involves promoting personal growth and well-being, leading to a more satisfying work experience for everyone.

Compassion and Corporate Social Responsibility (CSR)

1. **Improving Brand Reputation:** Organizations known for being empathetic in all aspects of business, including employee relations and community involvement, typically have a stronger reputation. Customers prefer to do business with companies that share their values, which can result in improved client loyalty and a stronger brand.
2. **Encouraging Sustainable Business Practices:** Compassion affects a company's interactions with the outside world in addition to its internal operations. Compassionate businesses are more likely to adopt sustainable practices that consider the long-term well-being of the environment and the global community.

Challenges of Implementing Compassion in Professional Settings

1. **Finding a Balance Between Empathy and Accountability:** One of the hardest aspects of incorporating compassion into professional life is balancing empathy with accountability. It is essential for leaders to show

compassion for their colleagues while also holding them accountable for their work.

2. Cultural Variations in the Expression of Compassion: Variations in perceptions can impact the way compassion is understood and demonstrated in international organizations. Leaders must exhibit cultural sensitivity and adjust their approaches to align with the diverse backgrounds of their team members.

Conclusion

In the workplace, compassion plays a crucial role in fostering productive, sustainable, and fulfilling environments. It is not just a nice-to-have. In addition to improving operational efficiency, companies can positively impact society by cultivating an atmosphere that values and practices compassion. This section has highlighted the various benefits of compassion in the workplace and provided a guide for managers wishing to foster a more understanding and supportive environment.

Strategies for Integrating Compassion into Daily Life

Introduction

Compassion integration demands deliberate effort and regular practice, particularly in a work environment. It is about integrating empathy and compassion into your everyday interactions with people, which may improve both your personal and professional lives in a big way. Here, we look at doable tactics that people and groups can use to incorporate compassion into all their daily encounters.

Active Listening

1. Engage in Full Presence Practice: Always pay close attention to the speaker. Keep your mind off things like looking at your phone or planning your reply while the other person is speaking. This shows that you genuinely appreciate what they have to say.
2. Promote Sharing: Establish an environment where colleagues are comfortable sharing their ideas and emotions. By posing open-ended questions that encourage in-depth dialogue, this can be promoted.
3. Reflect and Explain: Summarize what you have heard and provide clarification as necessary to demonstrate that you are paying attention. This not only guarantees accurate comprehension but also communicates to the speaker your importance for what they have spoken.

Empathy Exercises

1. Role-playing: Participate in role-playing activities that let you see things from the viewpoint of another person. This is notably useful in training sessions aimed at boosting emotional intelligence or in conflict resolution.
2. Introspection: Consistently consider the impact of your behavior on other people. Think about journaling about the people you meet every day and how you can respond more empathically.
3. Empathy Mapping: To better understand client needs or address internal problems, use empathy maps in team situations. This tool smooths the visualization and expression of others' experiences.

Volunteer Work

1. Individual Volunteering: Provide paid volunteer days as a means of encouraging staff members to engage in voluntary work. In addition to benefiting society, this maximizes the personal life of the workers.
2. Corporate Volunteering: Plan volunteer events for your organization that complement the goals of your sector or company. This can strengthen team collaborations and broaden the company's societal influence.
3. Skill-Based Volunteering: Help neighborhood groups or non-profits by using your professional abilities. This kind of volunteering can be particularly satisfying because it makes use of your main skills for a worthwhile cause.

Integrating Compassion in Decision-Making

1. Take Stakeholder Impact into Account: Keep in mind that decisions affect a variety of stakeholders, such as the community, customers, and staff. Decisions are made with compassion and pragmatism thanks to this holistic perspective.
2. Ethical Aspects: Always conduct business with the highest ethical standards. This involves acting with integrity, fairness, and transparency—all qualities that are indicative of compassion.
3. All-encompassing Policies: Create policies for your workplace that cater to the varying demands of your staff. This covers things like accommodating living circumstances, mental health support, and flexible work schedules.

Cultural Adaptations

1. Cultural Training: One of the most important components of compassionate workplaces is offering cultural competence training to staff members so they can comprehend and appreciate people from different origins.
2. Feedback Mechanisms: Put in place processes that let staff members voice their opinions about the working environment and make suggestions for improvements. To create an encompassment that represents the needs and values of every employee, this feedback is vital.

Conclusion

Practicing compassion regularly is a fulfilling endeavor that strengthens relationships both personally and professionally. Active listening, empathy exercises, volunteer work, and considering the broader impact in decision-making are just a few ways individuals and organizations can create an environment where compassion thrives. These tactics improve the workplace atmosphere and promote a friendlier, more compassionate environment.

Community Involvement as a Professional Strategy

Introduction

Incorporating community service into your professional approach is about more than just giving back; it is about creating a connection between your organization's or your own values and the larger community. This kind of involvement can enhance your company's reputation, build deep connections, and positively impact both employees and customers. Here, we explore how strategic community involvement can benefit both parties.

Networking with Purpose

1. Allying with Relevant Causes: Choose community initiatives and causes that align with your company's goals and values. This alignment ensures that your efforts are genuine and resonate with your stakeholders on a deeper level.
2. Relationship Building: Participating in community activities offers numerous networking opportunities with like-minded businesses and local authorities. These connections can lead to partnerships and collaborations that might not have been possible through traditional networking channels.
3. Improving Brand Visibility: Active involvement in community events raises your profile locally. This can attract new clients or customers who are drawn to businesses that demonstrate a commitment to the community.

Corporate Social Responsibility (CSR)

1. Integrated CSR Strategies: Develop a CSR strategy that aligns with the core business plan. This should include specific goals for community involvement and metrics to evaluate their success. Effective CSR programs can expand markets, attract talent, and drive innovation.

2. Employee Involvement: Offer volunteer time off or match employee donations to encourage employee involvement in CSR initiatives. Involving employees in CSR not only boosts morale but also makes them feel more connected to the organization's mission.
3. Reporting and Communication: Regularly report on your CSR activities and their outcomes. Transparent communication about these activities can enhance your company's reputation and demonstrate accountability to stakeholders.

Mentoring and Advocacy

1. Professional Mentoring Programs: Create or participate in mentoring programs in your community or industry. These programs can enrich professional networks and develop future leaders. Additionally, mentoring is an effective way to pass on knowledge and skills to the next generation.
2. Community Issue Advocacy: Advocate for issues relevant to your community or industry. This might involve supporting legislation that benefits the community, funding initiatives, or leading awareness campaigns. Advocacy positions your organization as a community leader and active participant.
3. Educational Outreach: Partner with educational institutions to offer curriculum development, internships, or workshops. This kind of engagement can ensure a skilled future work force and prepare students for real-world challenges.

Balancing Benefits and Commitments

1. Evaluating Impact vs. Effort: Continuously evaluate the outcomes of your community service efforts against the resources you have invested. This ensures that both the community and your organization benefit from your efforts.
2. Long-Term Commitment: Community involvement should be viewed as a long-term commitment rather than being a one-time event. Consistent participation can lead to more meaningful impacts and stronger community ties.
3. Feedback Loops: Implement systems to receive feedback from the community and program participants. This feedback can guide future efforts and improve the effectiveness of current projects.

Conclusion

When strategically aligned with goals, community involvement can significantly enhance an individual's or company's impact and reputation. By actively engaging in community engagement, businesses can improve society, create a healthy workplace, increase brand loyalty, and promote sustainable business practices. This section proves a framework for incorporating community involvement into a broader professional strategy that is both meaningful and aligned with corporate objectives.

Balancing Personal and Professional Demands

Introduction

Integrating acts of compassion into both personal and professional lives requires a conscious balance to ensure sustainability and avoid burn out. Managing these obligations while maintaining the standard of service in both areas is the difficult part. This section explores practical methods for maintaining balance so individuals can manage their personal and professional lives simultaneously.

Setting Clear Boundaries

1. Establish Clear Boundaries: Set boundaries that help distinguish between work and personal obligations. This might include setting specific work hours for professional duties and dedicating time for family or self-care activities.
2. Express Boundaries: It is important to communicate and establish boundaries with colleagues, clients, and family members. Clear communication helps manage expectations and reduces the likelihood of conflicts or misunderstandings about commitments and availability.
3. Flexible Limits: While clear boundaries are important, flexibility can also be crucial, especially in roles requiring significant care and involvement. The ability to adjust boundaries without letting them collapse can help manage unforeseen circumstances better.

Integrating Personal Interests with Community Work

1. Connect Activities: Choose community service projects that align with your values or areas of personal interest. This alignment makes participation feel less like an additional burden and more fulfilling.
2. Exploit Skills: Leverage your professional experience for community projects that benefit both you and the community. For example, a marketer could assist a non-profit with its marketing strategies, enriching both their professional and personal sense of responsibility.
3. Involve Friends and Family: Include friends and family in community activities whenever possible. This strengthens interpersonal bonds and shares the workload, making the activities more enjoyable and fulfilling.

Time Management Techniques

1. Prioritize Jobs: Use prioritization techniques, like the Eisenhower Box, to categorize tasks by importance and urgency. This helps you focus on important tasks and reduces time spent on less important ones.
2. Effective Planning: Dedicate time each week to plan your work, family, self-care, and community activities. A well-thought-out schedule ensure adequate attention to each area and avoids last-minute rush decisions.
3. Make Use of Technology: Use technology tools like task management applications and digital calendars to stay on top of obligations and deadlines. These tools can help with scheduling and serve as reminders for upcoming tasks.

Maintaining Energy and Well-being

1. Frequent Breaks: Schedule short, frequent breaks throughout your day to refresh both physically and mentally. This is eminently important for occupations requiring a lot of emotional labor.
2. Self-Treatment Habits: Establish a self-care routine that supports your emotional, mental, and physical well-being. This might include regular exercise, mindfulness practices, hobbies, or simply time along to relax.
3. Seek Help: Seek support when feeling overwhelmed. Peer groups experiencing similar challenges or professional services like counseling can provide support.

Conclusion

Balancing the demands of work and personal life with actively engaging in caring activities can be challenging, but it is achievable with the right strategies. Sustainable care involves setting boundaries, prioritizing tasks, balancing volunteer work with personal interests, and maintaining your well-being. By implementing these strategies, you can ensure that your efforts to care do not interfere with your professional obligations or personal well-being.

Long-Term Benefits of 'Afford To Care'

Introduction

There are significant and long-lasting advantages to incorporating compassion into both personal and professional spheres of one's life. 'Afford To Care' is more than just a philosophy; it is a workable framework that encourages a fuller, more satisfying life and long-term success in a range of endeavors. This section outlines the long-term advantages of implementing this compassionate strategy, emphasizing how it improves workplace settings, fortifies community links, and enriches the individual.

Personal Fulfillment and Well-being

1. Greater Happiness: Studies have shown a correlation between higher conditions of happiness and satisfaction and caring behaviors and community involvement. Numerous studies in psychology have shown that giving to others produces endorphins, sometimes known as the 'helper's high,' which boosts mood and general sense of wellbeing.
2. Less Stress and improved Health: Taking care of other people can result in less stress and improved physical health. Altruistic actions can lower blood pressure, lessen stress symptoms, and potentially lengthen life, according to studies.
3. Augmented Sense of Purpose: Giving to others on a regular basis inflates a more acute sense of meaning and purpose in life. This can have a particularly positive effect during periods of personal upheaval since it offers an external and community-oriented viewpoint.

Professional Growth and Workplace Advancement

1. Increased Team Cohesion: Positive team chemistry can be greatly stepped up by an environment that values compassion. Team members are more likely to collaborate, communicate clearly, and encourage each other's professional development when they feel taken care of and supported.
2. Higher Employee Engagement and Productivity: Organizations that put a high priority on the well-being of their employees and cultivate a positive work environment tend to see higher grades of engagement and productivity. Workers are more inclined to provide their best job when they feel appreciated and cared for.
3. Attracting and Retaining Talent: Organizations with a reputation for supporting an ecosystem of care and active community involvement tend to draw in more candidates. Keeping top personnel can be greatly impacted by this, since more professionals are looking for companies that share their values.

Community Impact and Societal Progress

1. Strengthened Community Ties: Participating in community service on a regular basis helps to build a sense of solidarity and support among community members. Given that vigorous networks are more resilient during stressful or emergency situations, this can be quite important.
2. Improved Local Development: People and companies can directly support local development projects by

volunteering and participating in other community-based activities. These could include initiatives for economic development, health care, or education, all of which can benefit the community in the long run.
3. Social Change Advocacy: Individuals and businesses who can 'Afford To Care' often advocate for social change by addressing systemic issues affecting their communities. This advocacy can lead to larger-scale legislative and social reforms benefiting more people.

Conclusion

Adopting the 'Afford To Care' mindset has immeasurable long-term advantages. Individuals and businesses that choose to incorporate caring into their everyday lives improve not only their own lives and workplaces, but also the greater good of society. This strategy promotes a society that is more cooperative, understanding, and compassionate where the advantages of caring are distributed and magnified among people and groups. 'Afford To Care' is fundamentally about choosing to live a life that actively appreciates and advances the well-being of others, leaving a legacy of positive influence and meaningful involvement.

Real-Life Examples of 'Afford To Care'

This section sounds out the life-changing potential of 'afford to care' via the narratives of those who personify the Good Vibe Gangsta. Each story not only demonstrates how the principles covered in this book may be put into practice, but they also demonstrate the incredible results that can occur when someone has the courage to go outside the norm.

Rafael Amaya: Championing Community and Youth Development

Rafa, a retired professional soccer player and an influential community leader, perfectly manifests the essence of 'Afford To Care' which is a fundamental principle uncovered in this book. As part of the non-profit's founding team at Goal Impact Foundation and its inaugural Executive Director & President, Rafa has dedicated his post-athletic calling to leveraging his experience and leadership to inspire positive change and development in communities and among the youth.

Rafa's journey in professional sports is marked by notable achievements and transitions. Born in Bogotá, Colombia, and spending formative years in the United States, he distinguished himself early on, earning the 1983 New York City High School Player of the Year award. After graduating from Long Island University, his soccer skills led him to playing in top professional leagues across the United States and internationally in Latin America and Asia, including stints in the Colombian First Division and Major League Soccer.

Following his retirement from professional soccer, Rafa did not step away from the sport; instead, he shifted his focus towards nurturing future generations. Rafa's true legacy began to take shape after he hung up his boots. His transition from player to coach and community leader was driven by a deep-seated passion for education and empowerment. Recognizing the significant power of sports, Rafa became a central figure in youth development, not only coaching young athletes but also nurturing their growth off the field. His efforts are driven by a firm belief in the power of education and sports to transform lives. He consistently uses his platform to promote social impact initiatives and community engagement, embodying the principles of caring and responsibility in every aspect of his life.

One of Rafa's most significant contributions was the creation of a professional youth academy in the Rio Grande Valley, South Texas. Starting from scratch, he built a program that not only honed athletic skills but also emphasized education, teamwork, and leadership. The initiative reflected his belief that sports can be a powerful vehicle for positive societal change, providing young people with the tools they need to succeed both in and out of the sports arena.

Rafa's past role as a member of the Board of Trustees of the Colorado State Soccer Association further accents his commitment to expanding the impact of sports through structured programs and initiatives. His ongoing efforts are not just about forming skilled athletes but also about shaping well-rounded individuals who contribute to their communities.

Over and above his professional responsibilities, Rafa is a devoted family man, consistently integrating the values of care, respect, and community involvement at home. His approach to parenting mirrors his professional ethos, emphasizing the importance of education, personal responsibility, and community service.

Rafa's story is a compelling example of how the principles of 'Afford To Care' manifest in real life. His dedication to improving the lives of young people and his commitment to community engagement are evidence of the boundless impact one individual can have. Through his actions, Rafa demonstrates how embracing care, compassion, and community can lead to substantial and lasting societal benefits.

His life reminds us that caring involves more than just goodwill; it requires action, commitment, and the courage to transform personal success into a tool for community upliftment. Rafa's journey from the soccer field to the boardroom and elsewhere demonstrates how one can truly 'Afford To Care,' making meaningful contributions that influence further than individual achievements.

Rafa's narrative offers you inspiration and a layout for how to meaningfully integrate caring into your life and work. His journey from a celebrated athlete to a community leader exemplifies how our passions and skills can be directed towards larger, impactful endeavors that vibrate with the core teachings of this book. By following in his footsteps, we can all find ways to 'Afford To Care' making a difference that extends limitlessly into the heart of our communities.

Here are Rafa's comments from our enjoyable Q&A session with him regarding the book.

Q1: How do you define 'Afford To Care' in your personal and professional life?

A1: "For me, 'Afford To Care' is about integrating compassion into every action and decision, whether I am on the field coaching young athletes or planning community development projects. It means making a conscious choice to prioritize human values and well-being over mere profit or personal gain. In my role at Goal Impact Foundation, this philosophy drives our initiatives to make educational and sports opportunities accessible to all, underscoring the idea that caring is not just an emotional gesture but a practical, impactful one."

Q2: Can you discuss how mindfulness has influenced your capacity for compassion and empathy?

A2: "Mindfulness has been meaningful in my life, primarily in enhancing my capacity for compassion and empathy. As a coach and community leader, being mindful helps me stay present and genuinely connect with people, understanding their experiences and emotions more deeply. This practice allows me to respond more effectively to the needs of others, whether it is mentoring a young player or navigating the complexities of community engagement. By being fully present, I can better appreciate the challenges others face and contribute to solutions that ring personally."

Q3: Can you share a specific instance where you faced significant failure, and how did being mindful help, you cope and learn from that experience?

A3: "A significant moment of failure in my voyage was during the early stages of establishing the youth academy. Despite thorough planning, we faced unexpected setbacks that nearly halted the project. During this time, mindfulness was preeminent—it allowed me to step back and assess the situation calmly, without being overwhelmed by frustration or disappointment. This reflective approach helped me identify missteps in our initial strategy and soon led to a revised, more effective plan that emphasized collaboration and community input. Through mindfulness, I learned that failure is not the opposite of success but a vital part of the journey towards achieving it."

Q4: What advice would you give to someone struggling to find the time and energy to invest in caring for others?

A4: "My advice would be to start small and integrate acts of care into your daily routine. Caring for others does not always require grand gestures; sometimes, it is the small acts of kindness and understanding that make an enormous difference. Also, recognize that caring for others also means caring for yourself. Ensure you are managing your energy and commitments effectively — self-care is not selfish; it is necessary to sustain your ability to help others. Finally, find joy in these acts of care; let them feed your spirit and remind you of the impact you can have."

Q5: How do you plan to continue integrating these practices of care and compassion into your future endeavors?

A5: "Looking forward, I plan to deepen the integration of care and compassion in all my endeavors by expanding our programs at the Goal Impact Foundation to reach more communities and by mentoring other leaders to adopt the Good Vibe Gangsta ethos. By creating an ethos of care within the organization and in our projects, we aim to inspire a ripple effect, encouraging other organizations and communities to adopt similar practices. Additionally, I will continue to support policies and practices that prioritize community well-being at local, national, and international stages, ensuring that the values of empathy and compassion are embedded in broader societal changes."

Conclusion

Rafael Amaya's journey—from the soccer fields of Colombia to the community parks of Colorado—illustrates a baffling commitment to the ethos of 'Afford To Care.' His approach, rooted in mindfulness, compassion, and a steadfast dedication to community development, serves as a compelling example for integrating care into personal and professional domains. Through his leadership at the Goal Impact Foundation and otherwise, Rafa continues to demonstrate that caring is an actionable, impactful choice that enriches lives and strengthens communities. As he moves forward, Rafa's ongoing initiatives and advocacy for inclusive and compassionate practices promise to further his impact, inspiring others to make a meaningful difference in the world.

Let us now examine another powerful case study from the mother of the authors of this book.

Rossi: The Compassionate Journey Throughout The Americas

Rossi's story is an enthusiastic medley of care, empowerment, and community involvement, embodying this chapter, from her early days in San Antonio, Texas where family and community were intertwined in her upbringing. Leading into her impactful work across Latin America and back in Texas, Rossi has consistently demonstrated what it means to be a Good Vibe Gangsta by using her skills and compassion to uplift others.

Her journey began with a passion for making a global impact, leading her to develop her Spanish language skills in Guadalajara, Jalisco and then to consider children and family empowerment programs there in México, in South America (Venezuela), and eventually in Central America (Guatemala). These experiences honed in on her ability to connect with distinct communities, laying the stones for her enthusiastic work in Texas.

Upon returning to her native Texas, Rossi took her commitment to the next level by focusing on empowering mothers and children escaping adverse conditions. She helped establish a neighborhood of transitional homes that not only provides shelter but also offers a pathway to self-sufficiency through education, community support, and holistic services. Rossi's approach is not just about temporary relief but about galvanizing long-term, sustainable change in the lives of the families she serves.

Here are some of Rossi's prime insights that can help you 'afford to care':

1. Empowerment Through Education: Education is a powerful tool for empowerment. Rossi's focus on providing educational opportunities shows how equipping people with knowledge can open doors to new possibilities.
2. Community as Family: Building a nurturing community environment can provide the emotional and social support that empowers individuals to thrive, mirroring the familial support Rossi grew up with.
3. Holistic Approach: Addressing not just the physical but also the emotional and spiritual needs of individuals ensures comprehensive care and healing.
4. Persistence in Support: Rossi's commitment to walking with women for as long as they need reflects the importance of persistent support in achieving lasting change.

5. Safe Spaces are Necessary: Creating safe, home-like environments is necessary for healing and growth, chiefly for those who have fled dangerous situations.
6. Dual-Generation Impact: Focusing on both parents and children ensures that the benefits of programs extend across generations, setting up a cycle of positivity and success.
7. Therapeutic Services: Integrating therapeutic services into support programs helps individuals deal with past traumas, assisting self-awareness and emotional healing.
8. Peer Support: Encouraging peer interactions through enrichment groups and events promotes shared learning and emotional support.
9. Wraparound Services: Across the board services that address various aspects of life—legal, educational, emotional—ensure that no need is overlooked.
10. Celebrate Community Achievements: Hosting special community events and gatherings helps cultivate a sense of accomplishment and belonging among participants.

Rossi's life story is a testimonial to the power of care and compassion. Her work not only transforms the lives of the individuals she helps but also enriches the broader community, making her a quintessential Good Vibe Gangsta. Her approach to caring shows that with commitment, empathy, and holistic support, it is possible to change lives and afford to care deeply, proving that the spirit of giving and empowering others is one of the most impactful ways to live a meaningful life.

Her remarkable journey through life has not only been marked by her professional achievements but also by her deep-seated dedication to her family. As her mother, brothers, husband, and in-laws entered the later stages of their lives, Rossi once again exemplified the qualities of a Good Vibe Gangsta by stepping into the role of caregiver with grace, strength, and unwavering commitment. This added layer of family care reiterates her role as a cornerstone of support and love, reinforcing her embodiment of the Good Vibe Gangsta ethos.

Embracing the role of matriarch as a mother to Jimmy and Joey, and a grandmother to María Alejandra, Rossi has not only nurtured them with love but has also instilled values of care, resilience, and community involvement. Her influence as a matriarch ensures that these values will be passed down, creating a legacy of goodwill and active community participation. Her inspirational leadership within her family, particularly during times of need, sets a powerful example for her children and granddaughter. It teaches them the importance of caring for each other and supporting one another through all of life's seasons.

By nourishing a home environment that is full of hope, accountability, and support, Rossi not only cares for her family but also teaches them the value of creating such an environment for others. This nurturing atmosphere is significant for the development of strong, compassionate individuals. Her story culminates in a powerful portrayal of a Good Vibe Gangsta, someone who not only spreads positivity but also actively constructs avenues for others to find their own paths to success and well-being. Her unyielding dedication to providing education, safe environments, and holistic support to mothers and children reflects an informed understanding of the critical need for care in encouraging societal change.

In her work, Rossi exemplifies the Good Vibe Gangsta ethos by leading with empathy, creating sustainable change, heartening community strength, empowering through knowledge, advocating for the vulnerable, and celebrating every victory. Rossi's approach to social impact is not just about the services she provides but the heart and soul she pours into every interaction. Her ability to generate and maintain good vibes, even in challenging situations, inspires all who come into her sphere of influence. As such, Rossi's life is an indicator of how adopting the Good Vibe Gangsta way can lead to significant, heartfelt impact, making her a true embodiment of the philosophy that caring deeply and acting fearlessly affords everyone the chance to lead a better, more fulfilling life.

Conclusion

This chapter has reaffirmed, as we consider the impact of compassion and community involvement, that true success is determined not only by our personal accomplishments but also by the positive impact we have on the lives of others. Now that you have a fresh perspective on life and know how to incorporate care into everything you do, you are ready to learn in the upcoming chapter how to leave your unique fingerprints on the world and make sure your legacy is both lasting and significant.

CHAPTER 4 SUMMARY

AFFORD TO CARE
This chapter explores how caring for others enriches our own lives and creates a more compassionate society.

DIAGNOSIS
In today's fast-paced world, individualism often overshadows the power and necessity of caring for others.

PROGNOSIS
Make a deliberate effort to incorporate acts of kindness and caring into your everyday life.

TREATMENT
Identify opportunities in your community where you can make a difference and commit to regular engagement.

REQUIREMENTS
Empathy, commitment, and a proactive approach to community involvement and personal relationships.

NEXT CHAPTER
Leave Unique Fingerprints

goodvibegangsta.com

CHAPTER 5

Leave Unique Fingerprints

Introduction

We have the chance to leave a mark—a distinct fingerprint that showcases our influence and character—in every decision we make, action we take, and interaction we have. The figurative fingerprints we leave on the world serve as unique markers of our presence and influence, much like physical fingerprints, and can be linked to a specific person. This chapter explores the idea of personal legacy and how our deeds can have a lasting impact on not just our surroundings but also on the lives of the people around us.

The Concept of a Personal Legacy

The process of leaving your imprint is not about big gestures or spectacular accomplishments; rather, it is about the accumulation of small, regular acts tied to your core beliefs and goals. It is about the way you lead, the novelties you contribute, the relationships you nurture, and the community efforts you support. All these components add up to a legacy that surpasses your personal engagement and continues to impact others.

Why Your Fingerprints Matter

Your distinct fingerprints are important because they reflect the influence you have had on the world. They bear witness to your presence, convictions, and accomplishments. In the workplace, they have the power to mold the domain of large companies and define your pathway. In a private setting, they can mentor your loved ones and uplift your neighborhood. Realizing the significance of these fingerprints is crucial for understanding how every action you take can add to a greater story—one that you are constantly creating as you go about your everyday life.

Legacy as an Ongoing Journey

Building a legacy is a continuous process that evolves with each decision you make rather than being a one-time occurrence. It is something you develop day by day, interaction after interaction, and it is not limited to the end of a career or the later phases of life. Understanding this can change the way you approach minor and large decisions, giving them a more focused and purposeful feel.

This Chapter's Focus

This chapter will dive into how to leave your fingerprints efficiently and consciously. We will look at how important it is to clarify your principles, make meaningful goals, overcome obstacles, and keep refining your tactics to make sure your legacy is alive and well. It will provide helpful guidance on how to leave a legacy that accurately reflects your identity and values, in both small and significant ways.

Conclusion

By the end of this chapter, you will see how every decision you make contributes to the legacy you leave. You will have the knowledge and resources necessary to ensure your fingerprints are not just unique but also lasting and positive. The imprint you leave can encourage development, spark change, and have a significant impact on your community, workplace, and personal life. Let us discover how you might accomplish this in a deliberate and significant manner.

Understanding the Concept of a Personal Legacy

Introduction to Personal Legacy

A personal legacy is the long-lasting effect and influence that a person leaves on the world they live in and future generations. An individual's values, beliefs, and behaviors are reflected in their accomplishments, relationships, and contributions. Recognizing the strength of your influence and purposefully using it to produce positive and enduring outcomes are key components of understanding a personal legacy.

Components of a Personal Legacy

1. Values and Beliefs: What you stand for is fundamental to your legacy. It consists of the values and beliefs you uphold and advance by your choices and deeds. Your moral and ethical standards are embedded in your legacy

because of these principles, which also shape the way you interact with people around you.

2. Achievements: These are the concrete successes you make in your personal, professional, or leisure activities over the course of your life. Professional benchmarks, creative endeavors, or any other accomplishments that leave a long-lasting impression on your industry or community are all considered achievements.
3. Relationships: The foundation of your legacy lies in the relationships you build and the way you engage with people. This includes professional ties with colleagues and mentees in addition to personal relationships with family and friends. Your kindness, guidance, and support contribute to shaping how others perceive you.
4. Contributions to Society: A major portion of your legacy is the effect you have on the community and the wider globe. This can be accomplished by charitable giving, public service, volunteer labor, or any other endeavor that boosts the lives of others and promotes positive change.

The Significance of Leaving a Legacy

Leaving a legacy is significant because it provides direction and meaning to your actions. Knowing that your life has significance beyond your physical presence and that your efforts will continue to have a positive impact on others long after you are gone gives you a sense of fulfillment.

1. Motivation and Purpose: Having a clear idea of the legacy you want to leave behind can be a powerful source

of motivation, encouraging you to take on tasks and make decisions that will have the impact you desire.
2. Inspiration and Influence: People can be influenced and inspired by your legacy, impacting how they behave and make decisions. Your influence can extend beyond your immediate actions through this cascading effect.

Strategies for Building a Personal Legacy

1. Think About Your Values: Take some time to identify and define your core principles. Consider how you currently live out these values and how you could better integrate these principles into your daily routine.
2. Create Impactful Goals: Make goals that will improve others' well-being in addition to your own craft and personal development. These objectives ought to push you to apply your skills and resources for the benefit of society.
3. Live With Intention: Every decision you make shapes the legacy you leave. Lead a purposeful life by continuously choosing choices that follow your values and help you achieve your long-term legacy objectives.
4. Share Your Journey: Keep a journal of your experiences and spread the knowledge and understanding you have acquired along the path. This makes your ideas and aspirations more tangible and actionable while also assisting others in learning from your experience.

Conclusion

Seeing and accepting the idea of a personal legacy can change the way you think about and live your life. It is as important how you choose to create that mark as much as the mark you leave. You make sure that your legacy is not just enduring, but also a strong force for good by identifying your beliefs, establishing goals that are consistent with those values, and leading an intentional life. You will discover how to put these ideas into practice as we go through more of this chapter, making sure that your distinct fingerprints do make a difference.

Developing a Vision for Your Legacy

Introduction

Creating a legacy vision involves deciding what kind of impact you want to leave on the world in the future. It entails giving careful attention to your legacy and figuring out how to make your present activities support your long-term goals. This section will walk you through the process of formulating a compelling and distinct vision for your legacy, so that each action you take will have meaning and effect.

Understanding Your Core Values

1. Identify Your Values: To begin, develop a list of your core values, or the guiding principles that guide your actions and choices. These could be leadership, compassion, inventiveness, or honesty. To comprehend the origins and significance of these values in your life, consider the experiences that have shaped them.

2. Set Values with Actions: Assess how well your present behavior reflects your ideals. Consider both your personal and work-related endeavors. Do your actions and your values differ from one another? The first step in associating your behaviors with your principles is recognizing these discrepancies.
3. Continuous Values Assessment: As you mature and gain more life experience, your values may evolve. To maintain the relevance and authenticity of your legacy vision, periodically review and reevaluate your principles.

Setting Long-Term Goals

1. Establish Clear Goals: Using your values as a guide, establish SMART (specific, measurable, achievable, relevant, and time-bound) goals that will serve as checkpoints on your path to leaving a legacy. These objectives ought to be demanding yet doable, and they ought to be directly related to the legacy you hope to leave behind.
2. Visualize the Impact: Forsee the potential outcomes of achieving these objectives. Who stands to gain? What is going to change? Clarifying the kind of legacy you wish to leave behind and using visualization to motivate yourself can be highly effective.
3. Make a Succession Plan: Consider how your objectives can be sustained even if you are not directly involved. This could be putting others through training, creating

reliable processes, or laying the groundwork for future work.

Incorporating Legacy Thinking into Daily Life

1. Everyday Decisions: Consider your legacy when making daily decisions. This could be choosing initiatives at work that support your principles or setting aside time every day for pursuits that help you reach your long-term objectives.
2. Influence and Leadership: Whether you are supervising a team, overseeing a project, or counseling a family member, disseminate your influence effectively. Consider the impact your choices and leadership style will have on the legacy you hope to leave.
3. Mindful Communication: Use your interactions to share your vision and beliefs. This encourages others to think about their own legacy while also reaffirming your dedication to it.

Documenting Your Legacy Vision

1. Draft a Legacy Statement: A legacy statement expresses the influence you hope to create, like a mission statement does. Putting this down on paper can help you organize your ideas and serve as a continual reminder of your goals.
2. Share Your Vision: You may improve and get support for your legacy goal by discussing it with others. Feedback from mentors, family members, or close friends can open

your eyes to new possibilities and motivate you to keep working toward your objectives.

Conclusion

Creating a vision for your legacy is a thoughtful process that calls for planning, reflection, and active alignment with your objectives. You can make sure that your mark on the world is not just one-of-a-kind but also influential by defining your legacy clearly, living your life, in accordance with this vision, and periodically evaluating your course. This method not only improves your personal life but also makes sure that your legacy will go on and inspire others long after you are gone.

Strategies for Leaving a Positive Impact

Introduction

Making a good difference in your personal and professional lives requires deliberate actions and well-thought-out plans. To leave a lasting and meaningful legacy, this section provides you with several doable strategies for improving your surroundings.

Professional Excellence

1. Dedication to Quality: Strive for excellence in all facets of your work. Ensure that every output you produce, whether you are developing a product, delivering a project, or offering a service, represents your lofty standards and commitment to quality. This raises the bar for others and improves your reputation in the workplace.
2. Diversification and Improvement: Continuously seek new and improved methods to work in your sector. You

can establish yourself as a trailblazer and thought leader by embracing change and encouraging others to do the same.
3. Ethical Leadership: Always act with the utmost honesty and ethics in both your personal and professional lives. Establishing a reputation of trust and respect within your sector can be achieved through ethical leadership.

Mentorship and Development

1. Encourage Others' Growth: Become an active mentor to colleagues, recent graduates, or local residents. Share your knowledge and expertise with others so they can also grow and thrive. Mentoring can have an extreme effect that goes afar the personal connections and advances your community or field.
2. Create Opportunities: Provide opportunities for others whenever you can. This could involve making introductions, endorsing someone for employment, or funding programs for education and training. Every act of empowerment contributes to the establishment of others' achievement, which is an organic element of a legacy that endures.
3. Set an Example: Model the attitudes and actions you want to see in others. One of the best ways to influence others and leave your beliefs on your team or in your community is to lead by example.

Community Engagement

1. Promote Active Participation: Engage in activities and events in your community. Your local involvement can make a significant impact, especially if it supports marginalized communities or addresses urgent needs.
2. Encourage Local Causes: Contribute financially or through volunteering to support local causes. In addition to helping the community, this assistance fortifies your ties to it, enhancing your significance as an important member of the community.
3. Push for Change: Make a significant impact on your community or industry by using your voice and position to advocate for change. More people will be impacted by your advocacy than by your direct action alone.

Balancing Personal and Professional Commitments

1. Integrate Ideals Across Spheres: Ensure your professional actions and your personal ideals are consistent with each other. Maintaining consistency in your behavior is crucial for creating a strong and cohesive legacy, and this integration helps you do just that.
2. Time Management: Make sure you have enough time to devote to your business and community obligations without compromising your personal well-being. Delegation and priority-setting tools can be extremely helpful in this situation.
3. Self-care: Take care of your physical and mental well-being to ensure you have the stamina to work toward your

objectives. Maintaining your capacity to have a good influence over time requires self-care.

Conclusion

This section's tactics offer a road map for anyone hoping to have a long-lasting good influence on both their personal and professional lives. You can make sure that your distinctive fingerprints not only define your legacy but also encourage and enable others to leave their own by setting an example, mentoring others, working toward excellence, and participating in your community. Recall that the whole of your daily decisions determines the legacy you leave behind, so consider the influence each one will have on the legacy you hope to create.

Facing and Overcoming Challenges

Introduction

Bequeathing a meaningful legacy is a lofty goal that will undoubtedly require facing and conquering a variety of obstacles. Your capacity to overcome these difficulties, whether they be social, professional, or personal setbacks, will determine how strong and long-lasting your legacy is. This section looks at how to overcome these obstacles so that your efforts to have a positive influence do not waver.

Common Challenges in Building a Legacy

1. Consistency in Values and Behaviors: It can be difficult to keep your declared values and regular behaviors consistent, particularly when you are under pressure. The

challenges of life often put our dedication to our values to the test.
2. Resistance to Change: Whether in a community or at work, resistance to implementing new ideas or altering current structures is possible. This resistance may be the result of miscommunication, anxiety, or ingrained preferences.
3. Resource Constraints: You could find it difficult to pursue objectives that add to your legacy if you do not have enough money, time, or other resources. Careful planning and prioritization are necessary to strike a balance between your goals and these constrained resources.

Strategies for Overcoming Challenges

1. Reaffirming Commitment to Key Principles: Review and reiterate your ruling principles on a regular basis. Especially in trying times, this exercise can assist you in bringing your behaviors back into sequence with your values. This reaffirmation might be aided by reflective activities like writing or meditation.
2. Communication and Education: Overcome opposition by informing people around you of the advantages and justifications for your actions. Successful communication has the power to change doubt into belief and challenges into chances for cooperation.
3. Resource Management: Make the most of your resources by forming smart alliances and managing them effectively. Acquire the ability to assign responsibilities,

look for partnerships that will increase your influence, and use technology to expedite procedures.

Adapting to Setbacks

1. Flexibility in Methods, Not Goals: When faced with obstacles, remain consistent in your goals but be adaptable in your approach to achieving them. Adapting your strategies to get around hurdles frequently results in creative ideas that you might not have thought of otherwise.
2. Seeking Assistance: Do not handle difficulties by yourself. Seek guidance and assistance from peers, mentors, or professional networks. Not only can a supporting network offer useful ideas, but it may also offer moral support.
3. Acknowledging Failures: See every obstacle as a chance to improve. Examine what went wrong and why, then make use of this knowledge to improve your next attempts. This helps you not only get through your current problems but also gets you ready for bigger ones down the road.

Maintaining Momentum

1. Honoring Minor Victories: Acknowledge and commemorate minor triumphs throughout your path. This keeps your projects moving forward and boosts the spirits of everyone concerned, including yourself.
2. Constant Improvement: Seek to always amp up your tactics and methods. Keep up with any new theories,

technologies, or techniques that can improve your efficacy.

3. Persistent Work: Recognize that leaving a lasting impression is a marathon, not a sprint. Keep up your efforts even if things are moving slowly. In many cases, persistence is the most important factor in making a big difference.

Conclusion

Overcoming obstacles is one of the most important aspects of leaving a legacy. You can overcome these obstacles by adhering to your principles, managing resources wisely, adapting to changes, and maintaining a strong support system. Every obstacle you overcome not only brings you closer to your legacy objectives but also reinforces your legacy by showcasing your perseverance and dedication.

Measuring Your Impact

Introduction

It is critical to have systems in place to assess the results of your efforts as you strive to leave your mark and create a legacy. Knowing how your actions are affecting others not only allows you to assess how effectively your endeavors align with your objectives but also helps you improve your tactics and increase your impact. To ensure your legacy is quantifiable and meaningful, this section explains how to monitor and assess the impact of your contributions effectively.

Establishing Metrics for Success

1. Establish Clear Metrics: First, decide what constitutes success for each of your objectives. Performance metrics for business accomplishments could include innovation rates, market penetration, or revenue growth. The number of people assisted, the improvement in community welfare, or the quality of personal relationships could measure the success of community involvement or personal relationships.
2. Quantitative and Qualitative Measures: To obtain a complete picture of your influence, use both quantitative and qualitative measures. While case studies, satisfaction surveys, and firsthand accounts can provide qualitative data, numbers and statistics can provide quantitative data.
3. Frequent Review: Schedule frequent times to go over these measurements. Depending on the nature of the goals, this could be done annually, every two years, or more frequently as needed. Regular assessment is necessary to keep your efforts aligned with your intended results.

Feedback Systems

1. Gather Input: Implement mechanisms to gather input from those impacted by your actions. Examples include direct surveys, focus groups, and open commenting on your digital channels. Feedback makes it possible to understand the effects of your initiatives in the real-world.

2. 360-Degree Feedback: Consider implementing a 360-degree feedback system in the workplace, which incorporates comments from peers, supervisors, and subordinates. This thorough evaluation can provide a variety of viewpoints regarding your impact and efficacy.
3. Community Engagement: Engage with direct communication with community members to better understand their viewpoints and experiences. Deep insights into the community's perception of your efforts and their true impact can be gained from this involvement.

Documenting and Analyzing Impact

1. Maintain Impact Records: Make thorough records of every action you take in relation to your objectives. Documenting both achievements and mistakes provides a historical record that can guide future strategies and help others learn from your experiences.
2. Make Use of Impact Analysis resources: Utilize programs and resources that can assist in analyzing the information gathered from your metrics and feedback. Clarity and insight can be obtained with tools such as social effect assessments, environmental impact assessments, or simply basic data visualization software.
3. Modify in Response to Findings: Be prepared to modify your plans based on the results of the impact assessments. If specific endeavors fail to yield the desired outcome, it can be necessary to change course or approach the issue from a different perspective.

Communicating Impact

1. Disseminate Results: Regularly inform relevant parties of the outcomes of your impact assessments. This could be newsletters for the local community, yearly reports for investors or funders, or team performance appraisals.
2. Honor Achievements: Openly acknowledge and applaud your initiatives' accomplishments. Recognition inspires not only the individuals involved but also encourages additional participation and support from the larger community or organization.
3. Acknowledge Your Shortcomings: Be forthright about instances where outcomes did not meet expectations. This openness helps credibility and trust and shows a dedication to ongoing development.

Conclusion

To make sure that your attempts to leave a legacy are successful and in line with your goal, measuring your influence is required. You can optimize the good change you bring about in both your personal and professional environments by setting up precise metrics, putting in place reliable feedback systems, and regularly evaluating and tweaking your strategy. In the end, these endeavors allow you to leave a legacy that is highly appreciated and felt by many.

Leaving a Legacy in a Digital World

Introduction

The idea of a personal legacy in the digital age transcends direct, in-person interactions and enters the virtual space. The internet, social media, artificial intelligence, and other digital platforms present special opportunities as well as difficulties for establishing and maintaining a legacy. This section examines the art of utilizing digital resources to fortify and augment your legacy, guaranteeing that your influence is felt both virtually and in person.

Digital Footprint and Its Impact

1. Recognizing Your Digital Footprint: Anything you publish, share, or engage in on the internet is part of your digital footprint. It can include digital photos, blog entries, comments, and posts on social media. Because the content you produce and interact with can have a lasting impact, it is important to be cognizant of it.
2. Consistency Across Platforms: Make sure your online persona lines up with your historic objectives and offline beliefs. By being consistent, you can strengthen your personal brand and make sure that all your online interactions are in line with your legacy's larger goals.
3. Managing Online Reputations: Keep an eye on and act on any digital content that is linked to you to actively manage your online reputation. You can monitor and control your internet visibility with the use of tools like reputation management services.

Using Technology to Amplify Impact

1. Social Media as an Influence Tool: Make advantage of social media channels to interact with like-minded people and groups, communicate your thoughts, and advance causes. Using social media to spread your message and reach a worldwide audience may be quite effective.
2. Blogs and Websites: Start and keep up personal blogs or websites where you may express your deepest ideas, chronicle your journey, and accentuate your accomplishments. These platforms can provide a more regulated space for sharing your heritage and expressing your ideals.
3. Digital Networks and Communities: Participate in professional and online networks that are pertinent to your objectives. Engaging in these virtual forums can increase your impact and assist you in gaining backing for your projects.

Challenges of Digital Legacies

1. Digital Permanence: The permanence for digital content to stay available forever can be both a benefit and a drawback. Errors or unfavorable information might also persist and possibly damage your reputation. Your internet presence can be routinely audited to help mitigate these hazards.
2. Privacy Issues: In the digital age, striking a balance between openness and privacy is of the essence. Exercise caution while disclosing personal information online and

be aware of the privacy options available on the platforms you use.
3. Misinformation and Misinterpretation: Your internet material may be misunderstood or utilized improperly. Posts should have a clear context, and you should communicate honestly to address any misunderstandings as soon as they occur.

Documenting Your Digital Legacy

1. Content Archiving: Keep a regular archive of significant digital materials, including papers, films, and correspondence. This preserves your work and gives others access to it in case they want to use your experience as a resource later.
2. Creating Digital Assets: Take into consideration producing digital assets that will be useful or instructive even after you are gone. These might be eBooks, educational films, or online courses that summarize your contributions and area of expertise.
3. Succession Planning: Make arrangements for your digital assets' future. To ensure that your digital legacy continues to reflect your values and objectives, you can include instructions in your will or estate plan for how your digital presence should be managed after your passing.

Conclusion

The digital frontier offers many options to create and project your legacy. You can ensure that your influence spreads widely and resonates in both the digital and physical spheres by carefully managing your digital footprint, using technology to amplify your impact, and addressing the challenges associated with digital legacies. As you proceed, keep in mind that every online interaction contributes to your legacy and is just as important as any in-person engagement.

Real-Life Examples of 'Leave Unique Fingerprints'

This section tells the stories of people who embody the Good Vibe Gangsta spirit, jumping into the transformative potential of leaving unique fingerprints. Each story not only demonstrates how the principles covered in this book may be put into practice, but they also show the marvelous results that can occur when someone has the courage to go against the grain.

C.R. Betirri: Cultivating Impact Through Art and Community

Betirri materializes the spirit of leaving unique fingerprints on the world through his consummate integration of art, culture, and community development. Born in Puebla, México, and now a prominent figure in Houston, Texas, Betirri's life and work are a verification of the power of embracing one's roots while contributing to the global montage of aestheticism and society.

Betirri's artistic journey began with a deep passion for sports and a personal challenge—his struggle with asthma, which prevented him from becoming a professional soccer player. After moving to the Bayou City with his family as a high school student and then double majoring in architecture and painting at the University of Houston, he discovered a way to combine his artistic talent and athletic passion into a single endeavor. Betirri channeled his passion for sports into his art, creating a celebrated series of paintings that depict bodiless sports figures in motion, capturing the essence and dynamism of athletes without focusing on individual identity. This unique artistic perspective not only features the universal nature of sports but also is parallel with Betirri's view of art as a medium for social commentary and communal identity.

His work, recognized and exhibited internationally, ranges from figurative to conceptual, always striving to evoke the spirit of his subjects. Betirri's role as the official artist of the Houston Lamborghini Festival since 2014 and his collaborations with major brands like Reebok Brazil and Major League Soccer mark his ability to bridge worlds—combining the vibrancy of sports with the introspective nature of fine art.

In addition to his artistic achievements, Betirri has played a far-reaching role in community development through his involvement with the Goal Park Foundation in Houston, Texas. As part of the founding team, Betirri has helped to transform seven blocks of the Columbia Tap Trail into what is poised to be a world-class park for the World Cup 2026. This initiative not only ameliorates public health and enjoyment through art and sports but also serves as a cultural hub that enriches the community and advances sustainable urban development.

Betirri's work is driven by a mission to bolster peace through understanding and healing through love. His approach to art and community involvement is deeply intertwined with his belief in the stimulating power of creativity and public engagement. By merging his architectural background with his artistic vision, Betirri has significantly impacted how communities interact with their environments, turning everyday spaces into arenas of cultural and social enrichment.

Throughout his trajectory, Betirri has been inspired and supported by many, but he credits much of his success to the foundational support of his wife, María Virginia Ivañez. Her belief in his vision has been a constant source of strength and motivation, helping him tread challenges and stay true to his path.

In this book, Betirri stands as a stellar example of how one can leave unique fingerprints on the world by integrating personal passions with broader social goals. His journey illustrates how challenges can be transformed into powerful expressions of identity and influence, inspiring others to make their mark through creativity, resilience, and community engagement. Betirri's story encourages you to pursue your potential to impact the world uniquely, reminding us that our backgrounds and challenges can become the basis for our greatest contributions to society.

We had the opportunity to conduct a Q&A session with Betirri, and this is what he had to say about the book.

Q1: What does it mean to you to 'leave your unique fingerprints' on the world?

A1: "Leaving my unique fingerprints on the world means behaving in the most authentic way possible. Doing things while believing that 'doing good' is actually the right path to do it, while breaking stereotypes and taboos."

Q2: How has being mindful influenced your understanding of your role in society?

A2: "Being mindful has led me to understand that we as humans are all different and we all have been raised in a very unique way. Being mindful creates a more empathetic approach to understand situations that are out of my control but that sometimes I can only have acceptance or learn from that situation to take a different approach in the future."

Q3: Can you share a specific instance where you felt your actions notably impacted your community or society?

A3: "This may sound contradictory, but in general, I think I have the privilege of being very humble and self-aware. There are two general examples that explain this: when I reach a certain milestone or achievement, I do not like to think that this makes me a better person than others. I appreciate the moment, and I feel it is a time to open up more to help or guide others. Similarly, when I go through tough situations, I like to think they are not permanent and happen for a reason, allowing me to learn, grow, or seek guidance."

Q4: What advice would you give to someone looking to make a positive impact but unsure where to start?

A4: "I believe that in order to make a positive impact, we all must start within our own selves. The moment that we learn the reason why we are in this world, we can authentically practice whatever we love, which will lead to a positive impact down the road. Start with you, take action every day and have patience."

Q5: How do you plan to continue making a difference, and how do you see your efforts evolving in the future?

A5: "In 2012, I decided to practice art professionally. I did not know how to do it and where to find help. I just felt that it was the right thing to do. Since then, I have taken action every day and this is what I will keep doing the rest of my life. I have a purpose, but I take action every day. This will make the difference rather than only dreaming to become an artist and not take action. Learning from my mistakes and accomplishments, I hope that I can be a good mentor for others that have the same purpose at an earlier stage."

Conclusion

C.R. Betirri's flight is an elated motley of cultural passion and creative expression, powerfully illustrating the impact of leaving unique fingerprints in both the art world and community projects. His creative approach to blending sports and art, coupled with his involvement in transforming urban spaces through the Goal

Park Foundation, underlines his commitment to making art accessible and meaningful within the community. Betirri's ability to draw from his copious background and personal challenges to fuel his artistic and philanthropic endeavors offers a compelling example of how creativity can be a force for communal and cultural enrichment. As he continues to expand his influence, Betirri's work remains a corroboration to the power of art in shaping spaces and narratives that bring people together and encourages a greater understanding of our shared human experience.

Now let us look at a case study that codes across continents.

Sergio Peña: Tech, Tradition and Transformation

Through his job-related accomplishments and life path, Sergio Humberto Peña Quintero typifies the essence of a Good Vibe Gangsta wonderfully. Born in Bogotá, Colombia, and educated in the United States, Sergio is now thriving in Japan, fusing technology, respect, and creativity to create beneficial effects everywhere he goes.

Sergio's varied cultural experiences are reflected in the complex menagerie of his academic background. He completed his Master of Arts in Classical and Ancient Studies at the American Public University System after receiving his Bachelor of Arts degrees in Asian Studies/Civilization from Baylor University and Seinan Gakuin University. His participation in Pi Gamma Mu and regular placement on the Dean's List, which attested to his academic excellence, laid the groundwork for varied and influential undertakings.

Sergio's professional journey, which took him from the US to Japan, demonstrates his commitment to using technology and education to improve people's lives. With his creative teaching strategies, he made a significant impact on both local education and international relations while working as an assistant language teacher in Japan. He transformed educational experiences in the United States at Alamo Heights ISD and Harlandale ISD in San Antonio, Texas, by introducing technology into the classroom and ensuring that students could access essential information through translation.

Sergio has developed his knowledge in social media and digital marketing in his roles as an SEO/Content Manager and IT Manager, increasing community involvement and brand recognition. Later, he started Peña Technologies and Takagi Digital, where he continues to push the frontiers of technological inventiveness and web development.

Sergio has dealt with and overcome linguistic and cultural barriers while residing in Japan with his wife and son. This has improved his quality of life and demonstrated his faith in the strength of family and community. His experiences support his belief that diversity should be celebrated, and that technology should be used to build relationships and change communities.

As a supporter of 'leaving unique fingerprints' on the world using technology for social benefit, Sergio embodies the Good Vibe Gangsta philosophy of optimism and positive change. His philosophy of technology is not limited to adaptation; rather, it aims to transform the way we communicate and form communities, making him a symbol of positive energy and significant change that is shared all over the world.

Fluent in English, Spanish, and Japanese, Sergio makes use of his linguistic abilities to improve his technical proficiency using progressive web development tools. Sergio's story is a powerful example of how one may live out the Good Vibe Gangsta ideology and leave a lasting, positive legacy on the planet. Sergio not only adapts to but enriches every place he touches with his passion for education, technology, and cultural interchange. He also serves as an inspiration to others, encouraging them to make a substantial and lasting difference in both their own and other people's lives.

Wrapping up our exploration of Sergio's striking journey, we reflect on a man who has effectively blended civilizations, technologies, and passions to leave a lasting imprint on the world. From the jubilant streets of Bogotá to the '09er experiences in San Antonio, Texas, to the vivacious energy of Japan, Sergio has embodied the spirit of a Good Vibe Gangsta by promoting inclusivity, leveraging technology for social good, and advocating for a world where diversity is celebrated, and unity is cherished.

We enjoyed the opportunity of a Q&A session with Sergio, and this is what he had to say about the book.

Q1: What does it mean to you to 'leave your unique fingerprints' on the world?

A1: "Leaving my unique fingerprints on the world means changing someone or something for the better, and having that change propagate down for years influencing others. The change in technology I did for my school districts in San Antonio nearly 10 years ago as well as the curriculum rewrite in the local Board of Education here in Japan I did nearly 20 years ago that is still in place and going strong is mind-blowing. It is also a genuine sense of pride and accomplishment."

Q2: How has being mindful influenced your understanding of your role in society?

A2: "As an educator, my role in society is influenced by mindfulness. A single thought, action or word can cause drastic changes, for better or worse. It is my responsibility to make sure I leave everything even better than I found it."

Q3: Can you share a specific instance where you felt your actions notably impacted your community or society?

A3: "My passion for technology and sharing my knowledge freely has led to a significant impact in my previous jobs. Even after more than a decade, the systems, tutorials, and training manuals I created are still used to train the next generation of educators."

Q4: What advice would you give to someone looking to make a positive impact but unsure where to start?

A4: "Ask yourself what would make your immediate surroundings better. Write them down. Then expand on those ideas. Why would it have a positive impact? For whom? How will it help? It does not matter how small it is because even a single pebble can cause an avalanche."

Q5: How do you plan to continue making a difference, and how do you see your efforts evolving in the future?

A5: "I will continue asking myself what I can do to help even a single person. I see my efforts being magnified by those I have helped, who in turn help others."

Conclusion

As we come to the close of our study of Sergio Humberto Peña Quintero's incredible journey, we consider a guy who has skillfully merged passions and technology to have a lasting impact on the globe. Sergio has personified the essence of a Good Vibe Gangsta by promoting inclusivity, using technology for social good, and fighting for a world where diversity is celebrated, and unity is cherished. He has done this from the colorful streets of Bogotá to the '09er experiences in San Antonio, Texas, to the animated energy of Japan. His commitment to community participation, inventive use of digital media, and unrelenting dedication to education highlight his role as an eloquent leader and a beacon of hope. Sergio's narrative demonstrates the ability of positive energy to leave a legacy that spans generations and borders in addition to being a tale of success in adjusting to new situations.

Finally, let us review a global case study from one of the authors of this book.

Joey: The Story of the Creation of VOS

Joey's creation of the digitally native VOS brand merges the spirit of entrepreneurship, sustainability, and social responsibility. VOS was not established as just a brand; it is a lifestyle that represents a balanced blend of international travel experiences, philanthropy, and wellness. Grounded in the captivating cultural heritage of Guatemala in Central America, the brand positioned the country as a Buena Vibra destination on the global stage, focusing on the uniqueness and positive attributes of the country.

Joey, an innate entrepreneur and a dual citizen of the United States and Guatemala, has always been inspired by his bicultural roots. This unique perspective shaped VOS, starting with its name, which is a nod to the informal 'you' in the Guatemalan flavor of Spanish, emphasizing a personal touch and connection to its roots. Initially focusing on eco-friendly natural rubber sandals, VOS expanded under Joey's guidance to include a broader range of travel services, apparel, and accessories, each piece reflecting his commitment to ethical practices and creative designs.

The brand's operations were purposely established to align with the United Nations Sustainable Development Goals, reflecting Joey's dedication to not just creating products and services but also promoting a global movement toward more sustainable and equitable business practices. His fingerprints were left on an international stage when VOS was recognized by the U.S. Embassy in Guatemala City and the U.S. State Department in Washington D.C. as a finalist for the prestigious U.S. Secretary of State Award for Corporate Excellence (ACE), acknowledging its impact and commitment to improving lives in Guatemala, the United States, and globally.

This accolade from the U.S. State Department highlights VOS' role in bridging countries and stimulating economic and social development through impactful, community-focused initiatives. Such as their partnership with Soles4Souls, which ensured that for every pair of sandals sold, another was provided to someone in need in the United States and Guatemala. Similarly, their partnership with the Gremial de Huleros and AgroSalud helped support hundreds of Guatemalan natural rubber agriculture workers and their families with health care, education, and improved living conditions.

Here are a few lessons from Joey's story that will help you 'leave unique fingerprints' as well:

1. Blend Your Worlds: Utilize your unique background to influence and innovate in your endeavors. Joey's dual heritage infused VOS with a distinctive character that roars globally.
2. Commit to Sustainability: Align your business practices with global sustainability goals to ensure that your enterprise contributes positively to the world.
3. Empower Communities: Engage local communities in your business model, whether through employment, healthcare, or education, to drive mutual growth and development.
4. Champion Transparency: Maintain transparency in your operations, especially concerning supply chains and labor practices, to build trust and accountability.
5. Innovate Constantly: Continuously seek new ways to improve your products and processes to stay relevant and responsible in a changing world.
6. Educate Through Action: Use your platform to educate consumers and other businesses about the importance of sustainability and ethical practices.
7. Celebrate Culture: Infuse your products with cultural significance that celebrates and respects their origins, enriching your brand's narrative and appeal.
8. Build Strategic Partnerships: Collaborate with organizations that align with your mission to amplify your impact and reach.

9. Focus on Long-Term Impact: Design your business strategies to create long-lasting benefits for both your customers and the communities you serve.
10. Lead with Integrity: Let your values guide your decisions; being recognized as a leader in corporate responsibility is a testament to acting with integrity and purpose.

The recognition of VOS by the U.S. State Department with a nomination for the Secretary of State Award for Corporate Excellence (ACE) is an example to the unique and impactful fingerprints Joey and his team have left on the global stage. This prestigious award, established to honor U.S. businesses that uphold high standards of responsible business conduct, placed VOS among an elite group of companies that are not only successful in their respective fields but also exemplary in their commitment to promoting social good and sustainable practices worldwide.

VOS' nomination for this award shines a spotlight on its dedication to bridging cultural divides and enhancing socio-economic conditions through progressive and ethical business practices. The brand's focus on community engagement, sustainable development, and cultural respect sets it apart in the fashion industry, particularly in how it integrates the United Nations Sustainable Development Goals into its core operations.

The Secretary of State Award for Corporate Excellence is one of the most prestigious recognitions a U.S. company operating abroad can receive. It highlights the importance of corporate social responsibility and sustainable development as crucial components of business success on the international stage. Companies recognized in the past include industry giants and innovators such as Coca-Cola, Citibank, Boeing, and Fruit of the Loom, each selected for their outstanding contributions to the communities they serve and for pioneering new standards in corporate citizenship.

The Global Cohort's Impact

The cohort of global finalists alongside VOS included some of the world's most respected and influential companies across industries:

- Coca-Cola in Romania: Recognized for its initiatives in water conservation and community engagement.
- Citibank in Brazil: Noted for its efforts in financial inclusion and literacy programs.
- Boeing in China: Acknowledged for its advancements in environmental conservation and technology transfer.
- Dole in Ecuador and Fruit of the Loom in Honduras: Both commended for their strides in improving labor practices and enhancing local living standards.
- Esso in Angola and Mars in Indonesia: Each exemplified for their roles in environmental conservation and developing sustainable agricultural practices.

This prestigious list not only highlights the significance of the ACE but also places the VOS brand in a league with companies that are leaders in their fields, recognized not just for their economic impact but for their unwavering commitment to improving global conditions.

Joey's leadership and the VOS brand's commitment to ethical practices, sustainability, and community empowerment have undeniably left unique fingerprints in the global marketplace. The recognition by the U.S. State Department serves as a compelling validation of VOS' efforts and places it on a pedestal reserved for those who are not only business leaders but also pioneers of positive change. As you consider the impact of these distinguished companies, let it inspire you to think about how businesses can be a powerful force for good, driving change that benefits not just shareholders but entire communities and, ultimately, the world.

Conclusion

As you close this chapter, remember that every deed and every interaction leaves a trace—your unique fingerprints on the world. Equipped with strategies to create a legacy of impact and positivity, you are ready to continue making thoughtful decisions that shape a better future. As your legacy begins to take shape, proceed to the next chapter to discover the rewarding experience of making splendid mistakes. There, you will learn how to turn every setback into a learning opportunity that propels you forward on your path.

CHAPTER 5 SUMMARY

LEAVE UNIQUE FINGERPRINTS

This chapter inspires you to make a lasting impact on the world by leaving your unique mark.

DIAGNOSIS

Many people struggle with the idea that their individual actions can make a significant difference.

PROGNOSIS

Identify your unique skills and passions and use them to create positive change in your community and beyond.

TREATMENT

Start small by implementing changes in your immediate environment and gradually expand your influence.

REQUIREMENTS

Self-awareness and courage to express your uniqueness in ways that positively impact society.

NEXT CHAPTER
Make Splendid Mistakes

goodvibegangsta.com

CHAPTER 6

Make Splendid Mistakes

Introduction

Many cultures and systems are deeply rooted in the fear of making mistakes, often interpreting them as a sign of weakness or failure. However, the key to innovation, advancement, and personal growth is to welcome failures as inevitable and invaluable teaching moments. This chapter challenges the conventional understanding of mistakes and setbacks, promoting an alternative viewpoint that highlights the valuable lessons and opportunities they present. We encourage you to rethink mistakes, push you to step outside your comfort zone, take calculated risks, and grow from the experience.

The Paradigm Shift

Historically, errors have been viewed negatively, as something to be avoided at all costs. This mindset can discourage experimentation, hinder creativity, and promote a fear of failure.

By changing our mindset to view mistakes as 'splendid,' we unlock new opportunities and insights. This chapter argues that when managed appropriately, errors can become valuable learning opportunities and milestones on the path to success and mastery.

Why Make Room for Mistakes?

1. Learning Opportunities: Errors are an honest feedback system that show you exactly what is wrong and provide you with ideas on how to fix it. Because they make us face complexity and challenge, they are frequently more educational than simple victories.
2. Innovation Drivers: Errors and unintentional discoveries gave rise to many of the greatest inventions and companies in history. We also give birth to unanticipated ideas when we give ourselves permission to fail.
3. Building Resilience: Taking responsibility for mistakes helps build resilience. We become better at recovering from setbacks by becoming more accustomed to managing them and returning stronger and more knowledgeable.

Goals of This Chapter

- Inspire you to reconsider your relationship with errors.
- Offer techniques for safely managing and making mistakes.
- Highlight instances where notable accomplishments resulted from early setbacks.

- Provide practical guidance on incorporating a positive outlook on errors into daily life and work.

This chapter will encourage you to embrace inevitable missteps, experiment fearlessly, and step out of your comfort zone as we explore the concept of making splendid mistakes. The goal is not to just make more mistakes but to make smarter, more informed mistakes that push the limits of what you believe is possible.

The Value of Mistakes

Introduction

While we often see mistakes as opportunities for failure and loss, acknowledging them as valuable learning experiences can change how we approach work and personal growth. This section examines the inherent value of mistakes, demonstrating how they are not only normal but also essential for success.

Learning and Growth

1. Direct Feedback: We get direct, often immediate feedback on our choices and behaviors when we make mistakes. In contrast to achievements, which could be the consequence of numerous uncontrollable circumstances, mistakes unmistakably point out areas that require improvement. Both professionally and personally, this input is priceless.
2. Deep Understanding: Often, a system's or process's failures teaches us more than its triumphs. Errors compel us to analyze the process, understand its elements, and identify problematic areas. This in-depth investigation

may result in a clearer understanding of how things operate and, consequently, lead to suggestions for improvement.
3. Evolution of Skills: Avoiding errors usually requires problem-solving and critical thinking abilities, which are decisive in both personal and professional settings. Every obstacle we conquer broadens our skill set and solves a particular problem.

Championing Innovation

1. Promoting Experimentation: People and organizations are more willing to experiment and innovate when the fear of making mistakes is eliminated. In every field, discoveries are rooted in this willingness to consider and experiment with novel concepts and methods.
2. Favoring Creativity: Errors frequently inspire us to produce novel ideas. In an environment where fear of risk is more prevalent, creative thinking may not have been stimulated by the modifications and solutions required to rectify errors.
3. Finding New Routes: Several scientific and technical developments came about because of unforeseen consequences or 'mistakes.' Researchers and business owners might find new avenues and answers by dissecting these errors, which may have escaped their initial attention.

Building Resilience

1. Emotional Strength: Emotional resilience is developed via consistently managing errors and coming to terms with them as a necessary aspect of learning. People grow more resilient and get a more nuanced understanding of both loss and success over time.
2. Adaptability: Every error is a chance to learn from it and react to unforeseen circumstances. In today's fast-paced environment, when conditions and requirements can change quickly, adaptability is rudimentary.
3. Perseverance: We develop perseverance, a major quality that successful leaders and innovators have in common, by continuing to try despite obstacles.

Conclusion

Recognizing the importance of mistakes is elemental for anyone hoping to advance, create, and lead successfully. We may change the way we respond to obstacles and failures by accepting mistakes as chances for growth and resilience-building. This section has emphasized the ways in which reframing our relationship to mistakes can result in more resilient, innovatory, and progressive people and organizations. Adopting this viewpoint equips us to maximize learning from each mistake and manage future errors more skillfully.

Strategies for Making Splendid Mistakes

Introduction

While it is clear that learning from mistakes is highly beneficial, intentionally incorporating them into strategies for professional and personal growth requires careful consideration. This section provides practical advice on how to make mistakes that are not only learnable but also fantastic opportunities for creativity, growth, and learning.

Cultivating a Risk-Taking Mindset

1. Normalize Risk: Begin by making risk more commonplace in your environment. Emphasize that taking risks is fundamental to progress, whether in professional or personal endeavors. Teach yourself and others the importance of taking calculated risks.
2. Promote Small Tests: Before implementing innovative ideas on a large scale, adopt a strategy of conducting small-scale tests or pilot projects. This approach creates a controlled environment where mistakes are manageable, and lessons can be applied immediately.
3. Honor Risk-Taking: Acknowledge and commend situations in which taking a chance yields insightful information, even if the result is unsuccessful. This nurtures a background that values and promotes taking risks.

Setting the Stage for Safe Failures

1. Provide Safety Nets: Construct mechanisms that offer backup plans in case tests do not work out. This could take the shape of contingency preparations, increased funding, or encouraging regulations that aid in managing the fallout from failure.
2. Encourage Psychological Safety: Create an environment where team members may experiment, share ideas, and discuss setbacks without fear of criticism or backlash. Lead by example: share your own mistakes and the lessons you have learned from them.
3. Lower the Stakes: Although taking chances is encouraged, it is a good idea to lower their possible adverse effects. Establish limits on the types of risks that are acceptable and provide precise standards for assessing them.

Encouraging Reflective Practices

1. Debrief and Reflect: After every assignment or project, hold a debriefing meeting to discuss what worked and what did not. Encourage candor and openness in these conversations to maximize learning.
2. Keep a Mistake Journal: Document the specifics of each error and the analysis that followed in a personal or group mistake journal. This is valuable for personal reflection as well as for helping others.
3. Adopt Continuous Learning: Make use of every error as a springboard for ongoing education. Promote continuing education and training that enables people and groups to

grow from their mistakes and use what they have learned to improve future performance.

Leveraging Mistakes for Innovation

1. Connect Errors to Ingenious Results: Examine errors methodically to see if there is room for creativity. Pose queries such as "How can we turn this mistake into an opportunity?" and "What can we learn from this error?"
2. Brainstorming Sessions: Hold frequent brainstorming sessions with the goal of examining errors and recognizing any discoveries or betterments that may result from them.
3. Create Prototypes Frequently: Prototyping is a valuable tool for iteratively testing ideas and providing practical feedback on failures. This can save time and money by allowing for iterative improvements to corporate procedures or product designs.

Conclusion

By implementing these tactics, people and organizations can change the way they see errors and start to view them as priceless chances for development and creativity. Making magnificent errors is about meeting obstacles in a way that optimizes learning and growth, not about pursuing failure blindly. Every mistake may be a glorious opportunity for both professional and personal growth if the proper mindset and habits are in place.

Appreciating New Experiences

Introduction

Making astonishing blunders often involves venturing into uncharted terrain and welcoming novel experiences. People can uncork their creativity, find untapped potential, and accelerate their calling and personal development by stepping outside of their comfort zone and familiar territory. This section looks at how accepting new experiences encourages taking risks and growing from errors, which eventually leaves a more varied and rich legacy.

Venturing Outside Comfort Zones

1. Frequently Push Yourself: Develop the practice of going outside your comfort zone. This could entail joining groups outside of your typical social or professional circles, speaking at public events if you are nervous, or taking on tasks that call for new abilities.
2. Establish Stretch Goals: Make objectives that will take you outside your present comfort zone. Stretch goals are audacious and force you to stretch your comfort zone. The process of achieving them promotes learning and personal development.
3. Acknowledge the Possibility of Failure: Realize that venturing outside your comfort zone makes mistakes more likely, but that is a good thing. Every error made in these new endeavors teaches important lessons that are imperative for growth.

Adopting a Beginner's Mindset

1. Develop Curiosity: Rather than approaching new challenges with fear, approach them with wonder. Being curious pushes you to investigate and comprehend novel ideas, which is pressing while exploring uncharted ground.
2. Cherish Learning: Develop a lifelong learning attitude. Take advantage of each novel encounter as a chance to acquire fresh insights, even if the result falls short of your anticipations.
3. Actively Seek Feedback: When starting a new project, get input from a variety of sources. Feedback can refine your learning process by offering viewpoints and insights that you might not have thought about.

Balancing Novelty with Expertise

1. Implement Current Talents: Look for methods to use your current knowledge and talents while attempting new things. This can serve as a basis for developing new competencies and lessen the uncertainty that comes with trying new things.
2. Integrate New with Old: Combine your current expertise with fresh insights and experiences. Generative ideas and solutions that advance both professional and personal development can result from this connection.
3. Record and Consider: Keep a record of the lessons you take away from novel events. You can better assimilate new knowledge by thinking back on past events and

figuring out how they fit into your entire professional and personal journey.

Creating Opportunities for New Experiences

1. Serve on New Projects: Offer your assistance on projects that go outside of your normal purview at work. This exposes you to fresh concepts and methods of operation that can sharpen your abilities and assess your way of thinking.
2. Travel and Explore: Take the opportunity to see new locations and learn about other countries. Your perspective can be greatly expanded, and new ideas can be generated by these experiences.
3. Ongoing Education: Participate in workshops or courses outside of your area of expertise. This broadens your knowledge base and introduces you to innovative ideas and perspectives from many people.

Conclusion

Embracing unique experiences involves more than just looking for novelty; it also entails creating a foundation for ongoing development, creativity, and adaptation. You put yourself in a position to make more intelligent, original, and absolutely wonderful mistakes when you push yourself further than your comfort zone, take on a learner's mentality, and combine current information with what you already know. These experiences improve your profession, enrich your life, and make sure that the legacy you leave behind is influential and ever-changing.

Learning from Outcomes

Introduction

Making splendid mistakes is only half the road; the other half is figuring out how to draw important lessons from the blunders you make. Simple mistakes become the ways and means toward increased wisdom and effectiveness through this process of learning. To make sure that every event positively impacts one's ability to grow both personally and professionally, we go into techniques for evaluating and learning from both triumphs and mistakes in this part.

Analyzing Failures

1. Objective Examination: It is important to conduct an objective examination of the circumstances following an error. Keep your emotions at bay and concentrate on the details, such as what occurred, why it occurred, and how it occurred. This objective examination can assist in identifying the underlying reasons for the error.
2. Examine Different Points of View: Contrasting viewpoints may exist regarding the causes of an error. Gathering different viewpoints will help you comprehend the topic more fully. This could entail talking about the error with mentors, coworkers, or other relevant parties who could provide ideas you had not thought about.
3. Record the Lessons: Following an analysis of the errors, record the lessons discovered. You should be able to access this documentation and perhaps distribute it to others who might find value in your experience. It is an

invaluable resource for training and growth as well as for preventing the same mistakes in the future.

Reflecting on Successes

1. Determine Success Factors: Understanding why things go well is just as vital as analyzing mistakes. Determine the choices, acts, or circumstances that made success possible. This has the potential to strengthen productive habits and approaches that can be used in subsequent endeavors.
2. Replicability: Ascertain whether aspects of your achievement may be duplicated and in what situations. By realizing the transferability and scalability of your effective actions, you may adapt these lessons to other situations and, if necessary, scale them up.
3. Celebrate and Share: Give credit where credit is due for accomplishments made by your group or company. Sharing success stories encourages a medium of learning and achievement by boosting morale and reinforcing the actions and methods that contributed to those successes.

Iterative Learning

1. Adopt an Iterative Mentality: Consider both achievements and setbacks as necessary components of the process. A fundamental tenet of continuous improvement and agile approaches is that every cycle presents an opportunity to improve and modify your strategy.

2. Establish Feedback Loops: To continuously collect information on the efficacy of your actions, establish regular feedback loops. Make wise changes to your tactics based on this feedback to keep them adaptable and effective in the face of shifting circumstances.
3. Continuous Improvement: Adhere to the kaizen, or ongoing, improvement, philosophy. With this strategy, you make gradual, tiny adjustments over time, always modifying in light of the lessons you take away from each endeavor or job.

Creating a Learning Ambiance

1. Promote a Learning Environment: Create an environment that values learning from both success and setbacks. Leadership that exemplifies this conduct and approaches that further continuous learning and introspection can also promote this.
2. Encourage Learning: Consider offering rewards to people and groups who effectively draw lessons from their experiences and put them to creative use. Rewards and recognition have the power to inspire people to participate fully in the learning process.
3. Use Technology to Enhance Learning: Support the gathering, examination, and sharing of lessons learned by utilizing technology instruments including digital learning platforms, project management software, and data analytics platforms. These resources can help your learning initiatives become more effective and widely distributed.

Conclusion

Whether they be triumphs or failures, learning from results is urgent to making wise decisions and enhancing performance in the future. You may help yourself and others make better decisions and avoid past mistakes by methodically evaluating, thinking back, and learning from every event. This increases your capacity to have a positive and long-lasting influence.

Real-Life Examples of 'Make Splendid Mistakes'

In this section, we study the exciting power of making splendid mistakes through the stories of individuals who embody the essence of the Good Vibe Gangsta. Each narrative not only illustrates the practical application of the principles discussed in this book but also showcases the remarkable outcomes that can arise when one has the courage to live in unconventional ways.

AJ Costa: Navigating Life's Twists with Resilience and Grace

AJ's professional journey epitomizes the essence of making splendid mistakes and harnessing them as catalysts for growth and adaptation. Growing up in the culturally rich hub of Houston, Texas, AJ developed a unique perspective on life and business, shaped by his exposure to a myriad of cultures and his upbringing in a family that greeted diversity with open arms.

AJ's life began in a home filled with love from two mothers and separately a father from Pakistan, ingraining him with a sense of inclusivity and an open-minded approach from an early age. This foundation laid the groundwork for his future endeavors, teaching him the value of seeing over conventional barriers and appreciating the unique stories of each individual.

From his early days post-college to his ventures into the cigar industry and upward, AJ has met each phase of his life with openness and the spirit of exploration, turning potential setbacks into instruments for growth. AJ's path has been marked by a series of roles that challenged him to adapt and excel across various industries. His specialty developed into being a SaaS Closer, Business Developer, and Storyteller, where he demonstrates an exceptional ability to build relationships and refine business methodologies. Each role has presented its own set of challenges, from navigating complex sales environments to pioneering new business strategies. AJ hails each challenge with a mindset that views mistakes not as setbacks but as opportunities to gain experience and innovate.

Colleagues and mentors frequently commend AJ for his ability to connect deeply with clients and team members alike. His approach expands conventional sales tactics; it is about creating genuine relationships that stand the test of time. His reputation as the 'King of the One Call Close' exemplifies his skill in sealing deals efficiently, yet it is his ongoing mentorship and support for his colleagues that truly intensify his leadership and commitment to collective success.

One of the most telling aspects of AJ's character was revealed through his respectful friendship building with Alex, the late father of the authors of this book, Jimmy and Joey, before he even knew of their relationship. This respect, given without prior knowledge of personal connections, points to AJ's intrinsic recognition of everyone's inherent worth and dignity—qualities in line with the Good Vibe Gangsta ethos.

The philosophy that "even the smallest of changes can make the biggest of differences" has guided AJ throughout his story. He knows intimately that life and business will not improve by chance but through intentional, positive changes. This mindset has allowed him to transform potential failures into lessons that propel him and his teams forward. His ability to remain patient, leave fears behind, and follow his instincts has turned numerous professional challenges into victories.

An avid traveler, AJ always uses his journeys as opportunities for personal and professional growth. Travel exposes him to a variety of business models and cultural perspectives, enriching his approach to entrepreneurship. Each trip is an experiment in adaptability—sometimes missing flights leads to unexpected local discoveries, and language barriers teach him new ways to communicate effectively. These experiences intensify his ability to connect with various audiences, an invaluable skill in all his business endeavors.

Perhaps one of AJ's most personal challenges has been navigating life with a birth defect called clubfoot, which causes the foot to be twisted out of shape or position. Instead of seeing this as a limitation, AJ has used it to fuel his resilience and determination. Learning to maneuver through life with this condition and doing so with a characteristic smile, has taught him the power of perspective and the importance of embracing one's unique journey with positivity and grace.

AJ serves as a prime example of how embracing and learning from one's mistakes can lead to enchanted personal and professional growth. His journey is a substantiation to the power of maintaining a positive outlook, embracing diversity, and continuously striving for improvement. Each challenge and misstep have been a catalyst for self-discovery and improvement, pushing him to adapt, grow, and eventually succeed in various aspects of his life. AJ's experiences serve as an indication for others, encouraging them to flag their own mistakes not as failures but as peculiar parts of the journey toward success and personal fulfillment. His story is evidence of the beauty of embracing life's twists with resilience, adaptability, and an enduring smile.

This is what AJ had to say about the book during our enjoyable Q&A session with him.

Q1: How do you perceive splendid mistakes, and how has this perspective influenced your personal and professional development?

A1: "Everything is a gift. I do not see mistakes as anything else except my ability to try at a thing and confidence that I can impact it. When I fail, it is just an outcome, not a lack of my ability. It is just an ability I do not have yet."

Q2: Can you describe how mindfulness has helped enhance your creativity?

A2: "It has been pivotal. I did not get into it as much until my 30's and am still on my journey with it. It has become more than a habit; it is something I know I need and go claim that space for myself each day."

Q3: Share a specific example where a mistake led to an unexpected creative breakthrough in your work.

A3: "I missed a meeting. Plain and simple. But I had been so attentive to the client, I think it was starting to feel more like pressure. By missing the meeting and just saying I got busy, which was the honest answer, it made the customer think they needed to value my time, and I was not their only priority. It made them introspective and instead of seeing me as a deliverable to their management, they saw me as a human who had competing priorities and treated me way better. It led to the deal getting done and at a quicker pace because now they valued my time too."

Q4: What advice would you give to someone who struggles to accept their mistakes or harness their creativity?

A4: "They are getting lost in the making of their own sauce. You cannot get mad when the sauce comes out wrong, you must keep making the sauce. Part of creating your signature sauce is making it different from everyone else and that only comes with trial and error."

Q5: How do you plan to continue embracing mistakes and creativity moving forward?

A5: "By continuing to learn and staying open to the gift of experience. We do better because we know better, and we only know better because we made mistakes. It is all a learning experience and if you handle every obstacle, mistake and suffering as a gift, you will find what you are supposed to learn from the scenarios."

Conclusion

The spirit of 'making splendid mistakes' is embodied in AJ Costa's approach to life and work, which shows how accepting obstacles and growing from setbacks can result in significant development and achievement. His capacity to bounce back and adjust is demonstrated by his journey from conquering personal setbacks like clubfoot to thriving in the fast-paced industries of sales and business. The journey of life is enriched, not by avoiding mistakes, but by accepting them as chances for creativity and introspection. AJ's narrative serves as a potent reminder of this. His unwavering dedication to self-improvement and community service motivates everyone around him to follow their own paths bravely and optimistically.

Now one of this book's authors has another compelling case study that we can examine.

Jimmy: Sailing Roatan Without a Compass

Now we will review a serendipitous mishap involving Jimmy on the tropical island of Roatan, located 40 miles off the northern coast of Honduras in Central America. Renowned for its pristine waters and abundant marine life, Roatan boasts some of the best fishing experiences on the world's second-largest reef, teeming with sport fish like tuna, mahi-mahi, and marlin.

Jimmy's adventure began when he reunited with a former soccer teammate, a local of Roatan, and another friend who was contemplating a real estate investment on the island. Their experience was far from typical; taken in by the local community, they saw the island through the eyes of its residents, not as mere tourists.

One evening, a family member of Jimmy's local friend invited them to try night fishing—a practice not without its risks, though the life-threatening dangers were unknown to Jimmy at the time since their boat had no lights. As they settled into the quiet rhythm of fishing under the starlit sky, their tranquility was abruptly shattered when another speeding boat bore down on them. In a moment fraught with danger, the locals quickly jumped overboard, leaving Jimmy and his friend to fend for themselves.

With little time to react, Jimmy and his friend instinctively maneuvered to avoid a catastrophic collision. Miraculously, the speeding boat soared just over theirs, narrowly missing a direct hit. This heart-stopping moment, while terrifying, ended with Jimmy and his friend safely rescuing their local friends and returning to shore, their lives intact.

This harrowing experience, while a splendid mistake, intensified their resilience and readiness to usher in the unknown. It even catalyzed the finalization of an excellent real estate deal, leading Jimmy's friend to invest in a slice of paradise.

Below are central lessons from Jimmy's experience as a Good Vibe Gangsta in Roatan:

1. Attract New Adventures: Life's richest experiences come from stepping out of your comfort zone and trying new things.
2. Cherish Local Connections: Building relationships with locals can transform an ordinary experience into an extraordinary one with deeper insights and authentic interactions.

3. Learn to Adapt Quickly: In unpredictable situations, the ability to think and act quickly can be lifesaving.
4. Value Teamwork in Crisis: The importance of trust and teamwork is magnified during crises; knowing how to work together efficiently can make all the difference.
5. Appreciate the Gift of Life: Close encounters with danger can deepen appreciation for life and the moments we share with others.
6. Turn Mistakes into Opportunities: Even risky or seemingly poor decisions can lead to unexpected opportunities and beneficial outcomes.
7. Cultivate Resilience: Overcoming challenges builds resilience and confidence, preparing you for future hurdles.
8. Keep a Positive Outlook: Maintaining a positive mindset in the face of adversity can transform a potential disaster into a learning experience.
9. Harness Fear to Empower: Facing and conquering fears can empower you to take on new challenges and expand your horizons.
10. Celebrate Survival and Success: Surviving a crisis and achieving a goal calls for celebration and reflection on the journey and its outcomes.

Jimmy's Roatan adventure is a perfect example of how, even in the face of danger, embracing the Good Vibe Gangsta philosophy can lead to personal growth, strengthened bonds, and unexpected success. Despite the unexpected and dangerous turn of events, Jimmy and his friend managed to steer through the crisis with quick thinking and teamwork. This not only ensured their safety but also reinforced their resilience and ability to manage high-pressure situations with a cool head—qualities central to the Good Vibe Gangsta ethos.

Moreover, the story emphasizes the importance of local connections and community-centric perspectives. By integrating with the local community and experiencing Roatan through the eyes of those who call it home, Jimmy and his friend were not mere tourists but participants in a shared cultural experience. This approach enriches travels and life experiences, reflecting the Good Vibe Gangsta values of respect, inclusion, and mutual support.

The successful real estate transaction that followed the night of near catastrophe demonstrates another significant aspect of the Good Vibe Gangsta philosophy: turning mistakes into stepping-stones for success. Instead of being deterred by the incident, they used the adrenaline and relief from their near-miss to seal a deal that would not have been possible without their initial decision to engage deeply with the island's life and its people.

This story emphasizes that making splendid mistakes is about more than maintaining a cheerful outlook—it is about actively creating positivity and opportunities from every situation. Jimmy's adventure in Roatan serves as a vivid validation to the power of positive thinking, the strength of community bonds, and the courage to pursue passions despite potential risks. These principles not only guide individuals through personal challenges but also encourages a supportive and thriving environment for everyone involved, exemplifying the impactful power of living as a Good Vibe Gangsta.

The closing of Jimmy's Roatan adventure brings to light not just the thrill and perils of exploring new territories, but also encapsulates the essence of being a Good Vibe Gangsta—turning challenging situations into opportunities for growth, connection, and positive outcomes.

Conclusion

Now that you have looked at the transformational potential of mistakes, you see that every mistake is a necessary step on the road to success rather than a side trip. You now possess both the bravery to try new things and the discernment to learn from every mistake, thanks to this chapter. Use this understanding as you enter the last chapter, where accepting the full range of experiences—both highs and lows—will be your biggest challenge and reward.

CHAPTER 6 SUMMARY

MAKE SPLENDID MISTAKES

This chapter emphasizes the importance of embracing mistakes as essential to innovation and personal growth.

DIAGNOSIS

The stigma associated with making mistakes often holds people back from trying new things.

PROGNOSIS

Cultivate a culture of experimentation where making mistakes is seen as part of the learning process.

TREATMENT

Actively seek new experiences where the risk of failure is present, and learn to celebrate these attempts, regardless of the outcome.

REQUIREMENTS

A shift in mindset to view mistakes as necessary for growth and a willingness to step out of comfort zones.

NEXT CHAPTER
Enjoy The Ride

CHAPTER 7
Enjoy The Ride

Introduction

Many people picture success as a destination, or a point on the horizon that we aim to achieve through diligence and determination. However, if we focus solely on the destination, we run the risk of losing out on the richness of the journey itself. 'Enjoy The Ride' is a plan for long-term success and a more contented life; not merely a plea to find joy in the trivial things. This chapter discusses the importance of maintaining a balanced perspective, appreciating the present moment, and finding joy in the pursuit of our goals.

The Journey Versus the Destination

In our society, results are usually valued more highly than the steps that led to them. This focus may result in a mindset that values goals more than anything else, placing less importance on the experiences encountered along the way. However, the path to every meaningful accomplishment is also the path to growth, learning, and fulfillment. Embracing this journey is crucial to preserving zeal and inventiveness, as well as preventing burnout that frequently results from an unwavering focus on results.

Why Enjoying the Journey Matters

1. Mental and Emotional Benefits: Constant pressure to perform well can have long-term negative effects, such as stress and worry. Enjoying the process reduces stress and promotes improved mental health.
2. Improved Performance: People are more engaged, imaginative, and productive when they enjoy what they do. Thus, enjoyment becomes a catalyst for better performance rather than merely a result of productive work.
3. Relationship Building: Success is rarely achieved alone. Deeper relationships with coworkers, mentors, and collaborators are made possible by valuing the journey because it creates a supportive atmosphere that encourages sharing.

The Goals of This Chapter

This chapter aims to shift your focus from solely achieving outcomes to also enjoying the journey toward these outcomes. We will discuss strategies to:

- Strike a balance between your personal and professional goals.
- Implement practices that enhance the enjoyment of daily tasks.

- Acknowledge and honor accomplishments, no matter how small.
- Adapt and prosper in the face of the unavoidable obstacles and changes encountered.

Conclusion

By the time you finish reading this chapter, you will have a better grasp of why it is so important to enjoy the journey—not just to keep yourself motivated and committed, but also to improve your life and the impact of your work. We will offer practical guidance on how to bring happiness and harmony into your everyday activities so that the accomplishments at the end of your journey are just as fulfilling as the journey itself.

The Importance of Enjoying the Journey

Introduction

While achieving objectives is vital, the journey therein needs to be given equal consideration and appreciation. In addition to improving our daily lives, having fun on the journey influences our long-term prosperity and wellbeing. This section explores the importance of finding happiness and fulfillment in the process and how it can improve our personal and professional lives.

Mental and Emotional Health

1. Stress Reduction: Stress and pressure can be generated continuously by dwelling on future objectives. Finding joy in small moments and acknowledging our accomplishments can drastically lower our stress and improve our mental health.

2. Preventing Burnout: Prolonged stress and dissatisfaction with daily tasks frequently lead to burnout, which can be avoided by appreciating the journey. We maintain a positive attitude and balance our energy use when we give the procedure some attention.
3. Emotional Resilience: We become emotionally resilient when we appreciate the journey and accept the highs and lows that come with it. This resilience helps us deal with problems more skillfully and keep a cheerful attitude when faced with hardship.

Reinforced Creativity

1. Openness to New Ideas: We are more willing to try new things and investigate novel concepts when we enjoy the process. Because it enables us to think creatively and unconventionally, this openness is a major source of creativity.
2. Constant Learning: A mindset of constant learning is stimulated by appreciating the process. Every stage of the procedure offers the chance to pick up new abilities and information that can be used to improve subsequent endeavors.
3. Enhanced Problem Solving: Enjoying the journey makes us feel more at ease and optimistic, which can improve our capacity for creative problem-solving. Individuals who take pleasure in their work are frequently better at solving problems quickly and creatively.

Building and Strengthening Relationships

1. Collaboration and Teamwork: Collaboration and teamwork are improved on delightful journeys. When everyone is enjoying the process, colleagues are more likely to have a pleasant interaction, encourage one another's development, and collaborate well.
2. Networking and Connections: Genuine professional connections and opportunities can come from interacting with people, attending events, and participating in activities that may not yield immediate results. All these things are part of enjoying the ride.
3. Mentoring and Assistance: Those with greater experience are more inclined to mentor others in a positive work atmosphere. In addition to helping the mentees, this encouraging dynamic gives the mentors a sense of fulfillment and purpose.

Conclusion

It is impossible to overemphasize the importance of enjoying the journey. It is needed for preserving our emotional and mental well-being, guiding variation and creativity, and reinforcing solid connections. We build the groundwork for long-term, satisfying achievement by living in the now and taking pleasure in the process. In this chapter, we will look at ways to apply this principle to everyday life so that the trip itself is as worthwhile as the goals we set out to accomplish.

Strategies for Maintaining a Balanced Perspective

Introduction

Maintaining a balanced viewpoint is crucial to enjoying the process of achieving both personal and professional goals. It entails controlling expectations, living in the moment, and making sure that work and personal life coexist together. This section provides doable tactics that will support you in keeping this equilibrium, enhancing your experiences, and encouraging long-term achievement without burning out.

Setting Realistic Goals

1. Fix Objectives with Personal Values: Make sure your objectives are in line with your own priorities and values. Being uniform allows you to work toward goals that are profoundly important to you, which keeps you motivated and committed.
2. Set Achievable Milestones: Divide larger objectives into more achievable milestones. Reachable benchmarks provide people with a sense of advancement and success, which boosts motivation and lessens overwhelm.
3. Modify Objectives as Needed: Be adaptable when modifying your objectives in light of changing circumstances or fresh perspectives. This flexibility prevents frustration and ensures that your goals remain relevant and attainable.

Practicing Mindfulness

1. Daily Mindfulness Exercises: Make time each day for mindfulness exercises including mindful walking, deep breathing, and meditation. By helping you focus on the present moment, these techniques can reduce stress and improve your general wellbeing.
2. Mindful Working: Incorporate mindfulness into your work by giving your full attention to the task at hand. Because it eliminates distractions and multitasking, this method can boost your productivity and satisfaction.
3. Reflective Pauses: Schedule regular little pauses to consider how you are feeling and how far along the task is. You may appreciate every stage of the process and maintain commonality with your overarching goals by taking these thoughtful breaks.

Cultivating Gratitude

1. Maintain a Gratitude Journal: Consistently record your blessings, even minor victories, and daily pleasures. This behavior cultivates an optimistic outlook by refocusing your attention from what is lacking to what is abundant.
2. Show Others Your Gratitude: Try to let friends, family, and coworkers know how much you value them. Relationships are strengthened by doing this, and it also makes you feel happier and more satisfied with yourself.
3. Honor Team Achievements: Whenever possible, in a work environment, recognize and honor team accomplishments. This approach sustains a healthy work atmosphere and a shared appreciation of the experience.

Balancing Work and Life

1. Make Time off a Priority: Ensure you take time off to truly unplug from work. Frequent getaways or days off help avoid burnout and enable you to approach your work with fresh perspective and energy.
2. Establish Boundaries: Make sure your coworkers and family members are aware of your clearly defined work and personal time limits. By adhering to these boundaries, one can prevent work-related stress from affecting one's personal life.
3. Partake in Extracurricular Activities: Regularly engage in fulfilling extracurricular activities, such as sports, hobbies, or social gatherings, which are unrelated to your job. These pursuits offer the standard counterbalance to obligations in the workplace.

Conclusion

Maintaining a balanced perspective is essential for both enjoying the journey and achieving long-term success. You may improve your daily experiences and accomplish your goals without compromising your wellbeing by setting reasonable goals, engaging in mindfulness exercises, developing gratitude, and striking a balance between your personal and professional lives. Putting these tactics into practice not only raises your quality of life but also establishes a steady pace that maintains your motivation and interest in your pursuits.

Finding Joy in Everyday Activities

Introduction

Finding happiness in routine tasks is essential to maintaining a positive attitude and enjoying the process of achieving your goals. It greatly raises both personal satisfaction and professional productivity by converting mundane jobs into enjoyable and fulfilling endeavors. This section looks at ways to bring joy into routine jobs so that they become meaningful and pleasurable even when they are routine.

Identify What You Love About Your Work

1. Pay Attention to the Passionate Aspects: Even if they are minor or sporadic components of your work, pinpoint the areas of it that you are most enthusiastic about. Try to increase the scope of these areas or add comparable components to more of your everyday chores.
2. Personalize Your Workstation: Add touches that make your workstation more aesthetically pleasing and indicative of who you are. This might include adorning the space with sentimental objects, artwork, or anything else that brightens your spirit and creates a cozier atmosphere.
3. Look for Meaningful Jobs: Try to do meaningful jobs more often. Look for ways to become more involved in certain initiatives or components of your work if they are more in line with your values or interests.

Incorporate Interests and Hobbies

1. Incorporate Personal Interests With Work: Try to include your hobbies and passions in your work life. This may be launching a blog for work if you enjoy writing or, if you are really interested in health and fitness, spearheading a wellness initiative.
2. Schedule Time for Interests and Hobbies: Make time outside of work for your interests and hobbies. Frequent participation in fun activities can boost creativity and invigorate your soul, both of which have positive effects on your line of business.
3. Use Hobbies to Unwind: Take use of your hobbies to unwind after a stressful day at work. Painting, hiking, or learning to play an instrument are a few hobbies that might help you decompress and keep work and personal life separate.

Take Breaks to Recharge

1. Take Regular Pauses: Establish a schedule that allows for quick pauses throughout the working day. Take a break from your work, go for a walk, focus on deep breathing, or do a quick relaxation technique during this time.
2. Take Mini-Detoxes: Every now and then, set aside a quiet day to detach from electronics and concentrate on non-digital pursuits that aid in mental and emotional renewal.
3. Modify Your Schedule: Occasionally switch up your daily schedule to avoid becoming boring. This may be as easy as switching up your commute, trying a different

lunch spot, or adjusting your calendar to make time for new experiences.

Mindful Enjoyment

1. Engage in Mindful Appreciation: Develop the mindfulness principle by intentionally appreciating the current moment and the task at hand. Mindful appreciation may greatly increase your satisfaction, whether it is through noticing the effort you put into a task or by relishing your morning coffee.
2. Honor Little Victories: Develop the daily practice of honoring and celebrating small accomplishments. Recognizing your accomplishments, whether they be finishing a challenging activity, making progress on a project, or just effectively managing your time, can improve your motivation and attitude.
3. Share Your Joy: Tell people about your everyday successes and joys, whether they are family, friends, or coworkers. Not only can sharing increase your happiness, but it also creates a pleasant atmosphere around you.

Conclusion

Sustaining motivation and enriching your life's journey requires finding joy in routine tasks. Everyday routines can become sources of happiness and fulfillment if you practice mindful enjoyment, take meaningful breaks, incorporate your interests, and focus on what you love. These techniques ensure that reaching your objectives will be just as fulfilling as the objectives themselves.

Learning to Pivot

Introduction

Being able to pivot or change course and approach in response to fresh information or unanticipated challenges, is an underlying talent for both professional and personal development. It involves adaptability, resilience, and the ability to manage change constructively. This section examines how learning the art of pivoting can enhance your journey by enabling you to gracefully handle life's uncertainties and maximize results.

Remain Flexible

1. Accept Change as Inevitable: Acknowledge that both the personal and professional spheres are subject to ongoing change. Accepting change as a necessary component of life can help you better position yourself to adjust to it as opposed to fighting it.
2. Develop an Adaptive Mentality: To cultivate an adaptive mentality, look for challenges and perceive them as chances to progress. This frame of thinking helps you to see unforeseen developments as opportunities rather than obstacles.
3. Lifelong Learning: To keep your abilities and methods adaptable, make a commitment to lifelong learning. This entails learning new skills, keeping up with industry trends, and investigating novel theories or approaches that can improve your flexibility.

Conjecture Change

1. Evaluate and Analyze: Give careful thought to the circumstances before deciding to change course. Examine the factors causing the shift and any possible effects they may have on your objectives and strategies. Your decisions regarding the necessary modifications will be based on this analysis.
2. Seek Contrasted Opinions: When things are changing, talk to experts, mentors, or peers who can offer fresh ideas or other viewpoints. This can assist you in gaining a better understanding of the problem and determining the best course of action.
3. Take Initiative: Try to foresee prospective developments and make backup plans rather than responding to them as they happen. By taking a proactive stance, you may manage changes more skillfully and keep control over the results.

Learn from Detours

1. Document the Journey: Keep a thorough journal of all the adjustments and difficulties you face, along with your solutions. For future reference, this documentation can be very helpful in understanding what worked, what did not work, and why.
2. Consider the Lessons Learned: After making a turn, pause to consider the event and identify the most important lessons. Think about how you can use these lessons in the future and how they could affect the way you make decisions.

3. Share Experiences: You can help and advise people who might be going through similar circumstances by sharing your personal experiences with others. By putting your learning into words, this not only strengthens your community but also your own education.

Conclusion

Effective pivoting involves much more than just responding to changes; it also entails turning possible setbacks into chances for expansion and creativity. No matter how many detours the journey takes, you may continue to enjoy it and confidently manage life's uncertainties by remaining adaptable, welcoming change, and learning from your mistakes. This section provides you with the tools you need to deal with life's unavoidable transitions with grace, joy, and balance.

Celebrating Milestones

Introduction

Milestones must be acknowledged and celebrated to keep motivation high and to value the process of reaching longer-term objectives. Milestones are important stops on your journey that serve as opportunities to reflect on your development and serve as reminders of your progress. To ensure that these significant occasions boost your motivation and sense of achievement, this section addresses the significance of identifying them and offers tips for properly commemorating them.

The Importance of Celebrating Milestones

1. Acknowledgment of Progress: Concrete proof of advancement is provided by milestones. By confirming that your actions are bringing you closer to your objectives, acknowledging them helps legitimize the effort you have put into your pursuits.
2. Motivational Lift: Individuals and groups alike can experience a notable increase in morale and motivation when accomplishments are celebrated. It offers a psychological boost that revitalizes all parties and reaffirms their dedication to the path ahead.
3. Reflection Opportunity: Every milestone provides a chance to take stock of the work that has been done and the lessons that have been discovered. Future activities and modifications can be informed by this reflection, increasing the efficacy of following efforts.

Strategies for Celebrating Milestones

1. Plan for Festivities: When creating your goals, do not forget to include scheduled festivities. Whether they are more formal events or more intimate get-togethers, planning festivities can provide extra incentive and something to look forward to.
2. Make Celebrations Wide-ranging: Make sure that everyone who helped reach the milestone is included in the festivities. In addition to making sure that everyone feels appreciated and acknowledged for their contributions, this inclusivity improves team ties.

3. Personalize Celebrations: Adapt festivities to the tastes of the people being honored. While some would value appreciation in public, others might favor recognition that is given in private. Celebrations can have greater meaning if these preferences are recognized and respected.

Documenting and Sharing Success

1. Keep a Success Journal: Keep track of all your accomplishments, no matter how small. This journal can be a source of inspiration during trying times and a personal record of your accomplishments.
2. Tell Tales: Tell success tales to people in your social circles or organization. In addition to spreading happiness, this encourages others to follow their dreams and recognize their own accomplishments.
3. Make Use of Social Media: Share achievements and festivities on social media channels. This can increase the visibility of your accomplishments, inspiring a larger audience and enhancing your reputation as a person or brand.

Reflective Practices

1. Review Goals and Milestones Frequently: Examine your objectives and the related milestones on a regular basis. This enables you to modify your plans as necessary and helps guarantee that your efforts stay in line with your goals.

2. Consider the Journey: After reaching a milestone, consider the path that brought you there. Think about what went well and what may be done better. It is important for ongoing professional and personal development to reflect.
3. Arrange future Steps: Make use of milestone celebrations as a springboard to organize your future travel segments. It is during these periods that one might take advantage of the momentum created by recent triumphs by setting new goals or modifying current ones.

Conclusion

Celebrating milestones is not just about marking achievements but about enriching the journey towards your goals. By recognizing progress, boosting motivation, reflecting on experiences, and planning for future success, you can ensure that your journey is as rewarding as the achievements that await you. This section has equipped you with strategies to effectively acknowledge and celebrate milestones, fostering a habitat of appreciation and continuous growth.

Real-Life Examples of 'Enjoy The Ride'

In this section, we explore the transformative potential of enjoying the ride through the narratives of those who embody the ultimate Good Vibe Gangsta. Each story not only draws attention to how the principles covered in this book may be put into practice, but also showcases the incredible results that can occur when someone dares to step nonadjacent to the conventional.

Brandy González: Navigating the Canvas of Life

Brandy's life provides a vivid illustration of what it means to 'enjoy the ride' in accordance with the Good Vibe Gangsta ethos. Her journey, infused with passion, dedication, and an unwavering commitment to art and education, reflects a masterful balance of embracing each moment while making meaningful contributions to society.

A native of San Antonio, Texas, Brandy's early exposure to the vibrant colors and rich traditions of her cultural heritage fueled her artistic passions and informed her unique aesthetic, which she expertly weaves into her work. Her art not only celebrates her cultural identity but also challenges viewers to engage with broader social issues, establishing her as a vital voice in the community.

Brandy's impressive and inspiring academic background, nurtured at prestigious institutions, significantly shaped her professional and artistic journey. She embarked on her higher education journey at Southern Methodist University (SMU), where she completed her Bachelor of Fine Arts, majoring in drawing and minoring in sculpture. Her time at SMU was marked by significant recognitions, including the 'Zelle Award' for outstanding artistic merit, which emphasize her exceptional talent and dedication to her craft.

Continuing her academic journey, Brandy furthered her education at Texas Tech University (TTU), where she deepened her expertise in the arts. Here, she earned a Master of Art Education, graduating with a perfect 4.0 GPA, followed by a Master of Fine Arts, specializing in printmaking with a secondary focus in painting. During her time at TTU, she received honors such as the 'Who's Who Among Students in American Universities and Colleges' and the 'Horn Professors Graduate Achievement' award, recognizing her contributions to social activism through the arts.

These educational experiences at SMU and TTU not only refined Brandy's artistic skills but also instilled in her an understanding of the moving power of art in education and society. Her academic achievements laid a solid foundation for her to influence and inspire as an educator, artist, and community leader, fully embodying the Good Vibe Gangsta philosophy in every aspect of her life.

Her academic achievements, underlined by a flawless academic record and multiple accolades, speak to her relentless pursuit of excellence. Yet, it is in her role as an educator that Brandy truly exemplifies the joy of the ride. By imparting wisdom and inspiring creativity among her students, she extends her influence beyond the canvas, nurturing the next generation of artists and thinkers. This role allows her to share the joys and challenges of the creative process, demonstrating how each step—whether a triumph or a setback—contributes to a richer, more fulfilling journey.

Outside the classroom, Brandy's commitment to her community is evident in her active participation in local arts initiatives and her efforts to make art accessible to all. Her involvement in workshops and mentorship programs reflects her belief in art as a vehicle for social change and personal growth, reinforcing the idea that to truly enjoy the ride, one must also pave the way for others to follow.

Her personal life mirrors this balance of joy and dedication. As a mother, Brandy integrates the values of creativity and resilience that she teaches at school into her parenting, fostering an environment where her children can thrive and embark upon life's journey with enthusiasm. Together with her family, she celebrates each day. Whether exploring artistic expressions or engaging in everyday activities, each moment is infused with the same passion and vibrancy that she brings to her work.

We had the pleasure of having a Q&A session with Brandy regarding the book and this is what she had to say.

Q1: What does 'enjoying the ride' mean to you in the context of pursuing and sustaining success?

A1: "For me, 'enjoying the ride' in the context of pursuing and sustaining success means actively building bridges rather than merely paving paths. This metaphor captures my goal of bringing people along with me in real time, cultivating connections and community as I progress in my career. While inspiring future generations is certainly a part of my vision, my focus is on making a tangible impact in the present—ensuring that each step I take includes others and contributes to our collective journey."

Q2: How has being mindful influenced your approach to balancing ambition and happiness?

A2: "Mindfulness has significantly shaped my ability to balance ambition and happiness by teaching me to prioritize and fully engage with the present moment. For instance, when facing deadlines or writing grants, I immerse myself completely in those tasks, dedicating my full attention to achieving the best possible outcomes within set time limits. This same principle applies to my personal life; when I am with my family, I shift my focus to fully engaging with my kids and husband. This approach not only enhances my productivity but also deepens my relationships, intertwining my happiness with theirs."

Q3: Can you share an example from your life where focusing on the process helped you achieve a better outcome?

A3: "In art, the unpredictability of the creative process is a constant reminder of the importance of focusing on the journey rather than the destination. For example, I might start a project with a clear vision in mind, but as the artwork develops, unexpected challenges or new insights often materialize, requiring me to adapt and engage in a varying dialogue with my creation. This ongoing conversation with the piece allows me to respond to what is actually evolving in front of me, rather than rigidly adhering to my initial concept. Embracing this fluidity often leads to outcomes that are more authentic and impactful. Trusting the process, is not just a practice—it is centric to the nature of my creative work."

Q4: What advice would you give to someone who feels overwhelmed by their ambitions and struggles to find joy in their journey?

A4: "My advice for anyone overwhelmed by their ambitions is to focus on taking the first step. It might sound cliché, but there's wise truth in the saying that a journey of a thousand miles begins with a single step. For instance, while working on a large mural recently, the scope of the project initially seemed daunting. I did not see a clear path to completion. In these moments, I focus on what I can do next—no matter how small. Each action, each decision, helps progress the project, allowing me to manage overwhelming tasks by breaking them down into manageable parts. Just keep moving forward, one step at a time, addressing each challenge as it comes. This method not only advances the project but also preserves the joy and satisfaction in the creative process."

Q5: How do you plan to continue incorporating joy into your journey towards future successes?

A5: "Incorporating joy into my journey towards future successes is all about maintaining a perspective of gratitude. I remind myself daily that the tasks I do are opportunities, not obligations. This shift from 'I have to' to 'I get to' transforms even mundane activities into moments of privilege. For example, when I think about household chores like laundry, I frame it as, 'I get to do the laundry,' appreciating that I have the means and ability to care for my family. This approach not only infuses joy into everyday tasks but also enhances my larger professional and artistic endeavors, allowing me to unite each part of my life with enthusiasm and gratitude."

Conclusion

Brandy González's story is not merely about the accolades she has earned or the positions she holds; it is about the vibrancy and joy she brings to every part of her life. Her ability to blend passion with purpose, personal achievements with community service, exemplifies a truly fulfilling journey. You are invited to draw inspiration from Brandy's example, to pursue your passions with vigor, and to impact your world in meaningful ways. Her life reminds us that the richest experiences come from embracing the journey, celebrating each moment, and spreading positivity wherever we go. She substantiates the Good Vibe Gangsta philosophy by showing that the true joy in life comes not just from achieving one's dreams but from the journey itself—embracing each experience, learning from each challenge, and always moving forward with a heart full of enthusiasm and a spirit ready to inspire.

Let us review another case study that connects the dots globally.

G. Jannuzzi: Global Grooves as the Cultural Conductor

G. is the true essence of a Good Vibe Gangsta, and his life is a masterclass in accepting life as it comes and radiating happiness. Thanks to his diplomat father, G. was born into a world that blended three festive cultures: Mexican, Brazilian, and Guatemalan. From an early age, he learned to recognize and manage diversity. He traveled across continents and communities because of this foundation, which led him on a lifelong journey of discovery and influence.

G. took in every lesson the cities he grew up in had to offer, from the busy streets of Guatemala City to the lively neighborhoods of Chicago, Illinois, and San Antonio, Texas. Summer trips back to Brazil and Mexico helped him connect with his roots and broaden his perspective, which enhanced his formative years. His destiny was also affected by this global upbringing, as he became fluent in four languages and acquired an intuitive capacity to interact with people from various walks of life.

G. considered education to be the most important aspect of his life, and he embarked on his higher educational pursuits initially in Austin, Texas and eventually in San Antonio, Texas, where he studied Finance for his bachelor's degree at UTSA. Then he went on to study at SUNY Buffalo's Brasilia campus to obtain a master's degree in education. Each academic pursuit was not just about personal growth but also about preparing to give back—a principle deeply ingrained by his family and experiences.

G.'s expedition is a montage of business and academic pursuits, with his dedication to uplifting youth at the center of each chapter. G. swiftly transitioned from his early jobs as a lawn care provider and JCC youth coach to positions that allowed him to mold young minds, including tutoring, coaching, and finally running educational initiatives and entrepreneurial soccer projects in Brazil and Mexico. His work has always centered around mentoring, utilizing education and athletics as effective means of maintaining both professional and personal growth.

Now residing in Brasilia, G. works closely with diplomatic communities to facilitate projects that benefit youth while also promoting social impact. His strategy is all-encompassing, combining global and local components to produce a harmonic effect and seeking to improve not just individuals but entire communities.

G.'s life mantra, "What do I do to inspire? Keep it real G," encapsulates his approach perfectly. He actively works to make the world a more welcoming, compassionate, and energetic place, rather than merely existing in it. Embodying the Good Vibe Gangsta mentality, G. navigates the waves of life's difficulties with the poise of a skateboarder and the enthusiasm of a surfer. He sees every obstacle as a chance for personal development and every conversation as an opportunity to share positivity.

G. demonstrates that the finest pleasures in life arise from the relationships we create and the differences we accept. He does not just enjoy the ride; he makes it unforgettable for everyone around him. His story serves as a powerful reminder of the transformational power of optimism as well as the advantages of leading an open and adventurous life.

We had the pleasure of having a Q&A session with G. regarding the book and this is what his feedback was.

Q1: What does 'enjoying the ride' mean to you in the context of pursuing and sustaining success?

A1: "To me, 'enjoying the ride' means embracing every moment of the journey, not just focusing on the end goals. It is about appreciating the assortment of experiences and lessons that come my way, whether they are challenges or triumphs. Growing up with a blend of Mexican and Brazilian heritage in Guatemala and the United States taught me to value each step of the way. Success is not just a destination; it is the culmination of the moments, connections, and growth that happen along the path. By staying present and finding joy in each experience, I sustain my passion and drive without getting bogged down by the pressure of achieving specific outcomes."

Q2: How has mindfulness influenced your approach to balancing ambition and happiness?

A2: "My ability to combine ambition and happiness has greatly benefited from mindfulness. It helps me stay in check and allows me to continue being conscious of my feelings and ideas. Instead of continuously pursuing the next big goal, I may better enjoy the little successes and lessons learnt along the road by being in the now. This strategy enables me to keep a balanced view of my goals and makes sure they enhance rather than diminish my general well-being. By encouraging me to stop, think, and acknowledge my accomplishments, mindfulness helps me maintain happiness and contentment even while I work toward more ambitious goals."

Q3: Can you share an example from your life where focusing on the process helped you achieve a better outcome?

A3: "One instance from my personal experience is when I worked on educational projects in Mexico and Brazil. My first objective was to witness noticeable, quick improvements in exam scores and program completion rates. But I quickly saw that concentrating only on these results was constricting. I was able to create a more significant and long-lasting influence by turning my attention to the process—forming relationships with students, comprehending their particular obstacles, and establishing a conducive learning atmosphere. Better long-term results resulted from this strategy, which not only raised the students' academic achievement but also their general development and participation."

Q4: What advice would you give to someone who feels overwhelmed by their ambitions and struggles to find joy in their journey?

A4: "I would advise them to take a step back and rediscover their motivation. Recall your motivations for embarking on this adventure and your personal priorities. Divide your objectives into more manageable chunks and acknowledge each little accomplishment as you go. Appreciate the experiences and personal development that come with the journey by practicing mindfulness and being present in the moment. Elect the company of people who encourage and inspire you. The most crucial thing to remember is to look after your physical and emotional health. Embracing the present and realizing that success is more than just getting where you are going, but also enjoying the path there are major components of finding joy in the journey."

Q5: How do you plan to continue incorporating joy into your journey towards future successes?

A5: "I intend to be loyal to my beliefs and passions to keep adding delight to my journey. I will continue to pursue my happy and fulfilling pursuits, which include mentoring youth, advocating for social impact initiatives, and building relationships with many communities. I will consistently engage in acts of thankfulness, reminding myself of the blessings in my life and the strides I have achieved. I also intend to keep an open mind and set about new challenges and experiences as chances for personal development. I will make sure that joy stays at the forefront of my road to future accomplishments by striking a balance between ambition and awareness, as well as by cherishing the people and experiences that add depth and significance to life."

Conclusion

G. Jannuzzi's incredible journey symbolizes what it means to be a Good Vibe Gangsta, fusing the colorful strands of diverse backgrounds into a life full of meaning and optimism. His narrative serves as a tribute to the strength of valuing one's background, utilizing knowledge to one's advantage, and making a commitment to the advancement of others, overall, the younger generation. G. has a talent for transforming every interaction into a constructive dialogue and every obstacle into a step forward, as evidence by his capacity to flourish in a variety of settings and his enthusiasm for bringing people together and inspiring communities. By keeping it real and spreading good vibes wherever he goes, G. inspires us all to cherish our journeys, enrich our communities, and, above all, enjoy the ride with open hearts and open minds, making a lasting impact in the most enchanted ways imaginable.

Now let us look at the final stimulating case study from the authors of this book.

Jimmy & Joey: The Flores Brothers' Life Journey

The story of these brothers is a vivid illustration of living life to the fullest, embracing both heritage and future with open arms. Growing up in a household buzzing with the rich traditions of their Italian-Spanish-Guatemalan and Irish-American heritage, they were constantly surrounded by stories, languages, and customs that spanned continents. Their parents, Rossi and Alex, and their grandparents, María, Carlos Enrique, Patricia, and Joe Edward, were not just family; they were the gatekeepers of rich cultural legacies that shaped Jimmy and Joey's identities.

Their early exposure to such diverse backgrounds taught them the importance of cultural respect and adaptability—a lesson that would serve them well as they traveled the globe, competing in international soccer tournaments and absorbing every new experience with enthusiasm and grace. Whether navigating the streets of a hectic foreign city or adapting to the challenges on the sports fields and academic classrooms, they have always maintained their connection to their roots, in which they drew strength from their ancestors' resilience and wisdom.

Their journey has also deeply involved caring for and respecting their family. Their dedication to their father during his battle with Parkinson's and dementia, and their ongoing support for their mother, exemplify their commitment to family values. They embody the principles of respect and honor not just in grand gestures, but in everyday interactions, providing a model of how to look upon family members with dignity and love.

Their sibling partnership extends beyond personal support to entrepreneurial collaborations, where they leverage their complementary strengths to create projects that are not only successful but also impactful. Their approach to entrepreneurship is marked by the same teamwork and mutual respect that defined their sports careers, proving that the strongest partnerships are built on trust, communication, and shared visions.

Here are some of their life lessons from their journey that can help you 'enjoy the ride' too:

1. Treasure Your Roots: Understanding and appreciating your heritage can provide a solid foundation and a sense of identity that guides your decisions and interactions.
2. Support is Strength: Having a reliable support system, above all in a sibling, can make life's challenges more manageable and its successes more enjoyable.

3. Honor Your Elders: Respecting and caring for family elders is not only a duty but a privilege that enriches your own life and strengthens family bonds.
4. Adapt and Overcome: Fix on change and challenges as opportunities to gain experience and learn, applying the wisdom of the past to the realities of the present and future.
5. Keep Learning: Whether it is a new language, sport, business model or cultural practice, continuous learning keeps life exciting and enriching.
6. Cherish Teamwork: In sports, business, or family life, teamwork can amplify strengths, divide burdens, and multiply successes.
7. Respect Differences: In a multicultural family, respecting and celebrating differences can lead to a richer, more comprehensive understanding of the world.
8. Balance Tradition and Modernism: Honor traditions while also being open to new ideas and practices that can enhance your life and community.
9. Communicate Openly: Maintaining open and honest communication in all relationships, particularly with family, prevents misunderstandings and builds trust.
10. Enjoy Each Moment: Life is a collection of moments; taking the time to enjoy them, regardless of the pressures of goals or expectations, can lead to a more fulfilling life.

In their adult lives, Jimmy shines as an incredible uncle, while Joey revels in his role as a devoted father to his only daughter, María Alejandra. Together, they weave a familial tapestry rich with support, love, and guidance, alongside the rest of their family and friends. As Jimmy imparts lessons of joy and curiosity to his niece, Joey provides a steady hand of nurturing and wisdom, ensuring that María Alejandra grows with a knowledgeable sense of her heritage and the endless possibilities that lie before her in the present and future. She stands as a beacon for the next generation, holding the torch that her father and uncle will continue to light and pass on. With this torch, she is poised to traverse life's journey with enthusiasm and grace, firmly grounded by the values that have been instilled in her. María Alejandra exemplifies the spirit of both enjoying the ride and staying rooted in the lessons of those who walked the path before her, ready to lead with vibrancy, firmness, and an open heart.

Their journey as brothers, athletes, entrepreneurs, and caretakers exemplifies the Good Vibe Gangsta philosophy of living life with enthusiasm, compassion, and resilience. Their story encourages us to savor the ride of life, with all its twists and turns, while holding fast to the people and values that matter most.

As you soak in Jimmy and Joey's story, let their journey inspire you to escalate your own heritage and the lessons of your ancestors. The strength to face life's challenges and the capacity to enjoy its journey are often found in the support systems we build, whether with family, friends, or communities.

Take a moment to reflect on the roots that ground you and the dreams that drive you forward. Like them, find joy in the ride—cherish each moment, seize every opportunity, and support those around you with the same fervor you pursue your personal ambitions.

As you move forward in your journey, ask yourself: How can I honor my past while forging a path toward a future filled with passion and purpose? How can I make my ride through life not just successful but meaningful?

Let this story remind you that life is not just about the destination but the journey. Relish it fully, live it deeply, and ride it with the positive energy of a Good Vibe Gangsta. Stand as if you have hundreds of ancestors behind you, and step forward with the courage to make your mark, just as Jimmy and Joey have done. Together, let us make every journey a ride worth commemorating!

Conclusion

As you reach the end of this chapter, and naturally our journey together, you have learned to savor each moment and navigate life's twists and turns with grace and enthusiasm. This chapter has celebrated the journey and prepared you to continue your adventure with joy and resilience. As you turn the final pages, remember that the true reward lies in the journey itself, enriched by each step you take with a Good Vibe Gangsta spirit, always pushing toward new horizons and achievements!

GOOD VIBES

CHAPTER 7 SUMMARY

ENJOY THE RIDE
This final chapter encourages you to appreciate life's journey, focusing on joy and fulfillment rather than just outcomes.

DIAGNOSIS
Many people are so focused on goals that they miss the joy of the experiences leading to those achievements.

PROGNOSIS
Adopt mindfulness practices that help you stay present and find joy in the everyday moments.

TREATMENT
Incorporate daily practices of gratitude and mindfulness to enhance enjoyment of life's journey.

REQUIREMENTS
Commitment to living in the moment and appreciating life's small pleasures as much as the big milestones.

FINAL CHAPTER

CONCLUSION

Recap of the Good Vibe Gangsta Principles

As we conclude our journey through this book, let us briefly revisit each principle we have uncovered, reflecting on how they can transform your approach to life and work:

1. Maintain Youthful Energy: We began by tapping into the vibrancy and limitless potential that comes with youthful enthusiasm, regardless of your age. This principle encourages you to maintain a spirited outlook, fostering innovation and a proactive approach to challenges.
2. Pursue Passions: Next, we explored the importance of identifying and relentlessly pursuing your calling. This principle is about aligning your professional life with your deepest passions and values, ensuring that your work is not only fulfilling but also impactful.
3. Accept Failure: Embracing failure as an inevitable step on the path to success allows you to grow and learn from each setback. This principle teaches resilience and the ability to turn every failure into a stepping stone toward your goals.
4. Afford To Care: We then explored the significance of compassion in leadership and life. Caring for others and actively engaging in your community not only enriches your life but also amplifies your impact on the world.
5. Leave Unique Fingerprints: This principle encourages you to make a mark on the world that reflects your

personal values and achievements. It is about ensuring that your legacy is intentional and uniquely yours.
6. Make Splendid Mistakes: Here, we learned to see mistakes as valuable learning opportunities. This principle emphasizes the importance of taking risks and embracing the lessons that come from unexpected outcomes.
7. Enjoy The Ride: Finally, we discussed the importance of enjoying the process, not just the outcomes. This principle is crucial for maintaining balance and ensuring that your journey toward success is sustainable and joyful.

Reinforcing the Main Themes

Throughout this book, the recurring themes of resilience, uniqueness, and positive impact weave together the seven principles. Each principle is designed not only to guide you toward personal and professional success but also to encourage a broader perspective on how individual actions can influence others and contribute to the greater good.

- Resilience is built through accepting failure, making mistakes, and continuously adapting to new challenges.
- Novelties spring from pursuing your calling, embracing youthful energy, and learning from every situation.
- Positive Impact is achieved by caring for others, leaving your unique fingerprints, and enjoying the journey each day.

Inspiration for Daily Integration

To truly benefit from these principles, integrate them into your daily life:

1. Set Daily Intentions: Start each day by setting intentions that reflect one or more of these principles. Whether it is tackling a project with youthful energy, taking a moment to care for a colleague, or reflecting on the lessons from any setbacks you encounter, let these principles guide your daily actions.
2. Reflect Regularly: Take time each week to reflect on how well you are embodying these principles. Are there areas where you could improve? Celebrate your successes and plan how you can better integrate these principles in the coming days.
3. Create Accountability: Share your goals related to these principles with a friend, mentor, or peer group. Accountability can greatly strengthen your commitment and provide you with support and feedback along the way.
4. Practice Mindfulness: Use mindfulness to stay present and aware of how you are applying these principles throughout your day. This can help you make more conscious decisions that align with your desired legacy.

Final Thoughts

As we close the pages of this book, it is important to reflect not just on the individual principles but on the overarching message they collectively convey. This message is one of empowerment, positivity, and transformation—not just of oneself but also of the communities and environments we each touch.

Empowerment Through Action

The principles discussed in this book are designed to empower you to take control of your life and your impact on the world. They encourage you to step out of passivity, to actively shape your reality through your decisions, actions, and interactions. Each principle, from embracing youthful energy to enjoying the ride, offers a strategic approach to living that enhances both personal satisfaction and professional success.

Positivity as a Force for Change

At the heart of being a Good Vibe Gangsta lies the power of positivity. This is not about ignoring challenges or glossing over problems—it is about approaching life with a mindset that promotes constructive outcomes and solutions. Positivity influences not only your own well-being but also inspires those around you. It is contagious and has the incredible ability to transform environments, turning challenges into opportunities and setbacks into learning moments.

Transformation Beyond the Individual

While personal development is a significant focus, the true measure of these principles lies in their ability to impact others. Whether through caring deeply, leaving a unique mark on the world, or learning from mistakes, the aim is to foster a broader transformation that betters our communities and societies. Your journey thus becomes a shared narrative, where your growth contributes to the collective advancement.

A Call to Integrate and Inspire

Integrating these principles into daily life is just the beginning. The real journey unfolds as you inspire others to champion these principles. Share your experiences, mentor others, and demonstrate through your actions how these principles can lead to a fuller, more rewarding life. The ripple effects of your efforts can initiate waves of positive change far beyond your immediate sphere.

Sustaining the Journey

Applying these principles is not a one-time task but a continual process of growth and adjustment. Life will inevitably present new challenges and lessons, and sustaining your commitment to these principles requires resilience and adaptability. Stay committed to learning, growing, and enjoying every part of the journey, no matter how winding the path may seem.

Embracing the Legacy

Over time, what you leave behind—your legacy—will be shaped by how well you have lived according to these principles. It is about creating a story worth telling—one that others can learn from, find inspiration in, and aspire to emulate. Your legacy is defined not just by what you achieve but by how you have influenced and uplifted others along the way.

Conclusion

This book provides you with more than just principles; it is a call to live deeply, love freely, and impact positively. It encourages you to live boldly, lead with compassion, and make a meaningful impact on the world. As you integrate these principles into your life, remember that each day presents a new opportunity to refine these practices and shape the legacy you will leave behind. Let the good vibes you create reverberate long into the future, leaving a legacy that is both inspiring and enduring. Here is to your journey—may it be triumphant, purposeful, and thoroughly enjoyable!

END NOTES

Book Cover Recognitions Cited

1. Department of State United States of America, *Secretary's Award for Corporate Excellence*, (U.S. Embassy Guatemala City, Guatemala, 2013)

2. The Wall Street Journal, *Digital Publication*, https://www.wsj.com/articles/SB10001424052702304096104579238690982515198, 2013)

3. The Rockefeller Foundation, *3S Awards Global Sourcing Council*, (New York, New York, 2012)

AFTERWORD

A Journey of Discovery and Transformation

As we close this book, we, Jimmy and Joey, want to reflect on our journey—not just through authoring this book, but through the experiences that have shaped us both as individuals and brothers on a shared path.

Authoring this book has been deeply meaningful for us. It allowed us to delve into our own lives, examining the lessons we have learned from our adventures and challenges. Each page, each principle, has been an opportunity to share our insights and a moment of introspection and personal growth.

Growth Through Every Chapter

From the inception of the Good Vibe Gangsta concept at a historic commencement speech to the development of each chapter, we have grown. We revisited our roots—our days at Texas Lutheran University, our travels, our entrepreneurial ventures, and our deepest passions. This journey reminded us that writing is as much about imparting knowledge to others as it is about discovering ourselves.

With every chapter, we reconnected with our core beliefs and the importance of positivity, resilience, and community impact. We saw firsthand how embracing one's true calling, as we have with this book, can lead to fulfillment and joy.

A Final Message to Our Readers

To our readers, we extend our deepest gratitude. Your engagement with *Awaken Your Good Vibe Gangsta* is not just about reading a book—it is about joining a movement towards a life filled with purpose, passion, and positivity.

We hope the principles we have shared will serve as guideposts on your path, guiding you to achieve your dreams and inspire and uplift those around you. Remember, being a Good Vibe Gangsta is about more than individual success; it is about creating waves of positive change that ripple through communities and generations.

As you continue your journey, we encourage you to hold onto the energy and insights from this book. Let them fuel your actions and decisions. Keep pushing boundaries, challenging the status quo, and most importantly, keep spreading those good vibes.

Continuing the Conversation

Our conversation does not end here. We invite you to stay connected with us and with the community of readers who are all embarking on this journey to awaken their Good Vibe Gangsta. Share your stories, successes, and challenges. Together, as a community, we can support each other and amplify our impact.

In closing, we leave you with the simple yet powerful epigraph that our late Italian-Guatemalan grandmother instilled in us: "You may not be able to change the entire world, but you can definitely change the world around you." It is up to each of us to seize every opportunity and make the most of it.

Thank you for being a part of this journey. Let us continue to grow, inspire, and lead with kindness, courage, and, of course, good vibes.

With gratitude and warm greetings,

The Flores Brothers

ABOUT THE AUTHORS

About Jimmy

Jimmy's biography reads like a visual odyssey—a journey captured through the lens of his camera, reflecting a deep understanding of human emotion and cultural authenticity. He is a charismatic global citizen whose career spans various roles, including that of Chief Operating Officer, consistently exemplifying the Good Vibe Gangsta spirit. His entrepreneurial experiences are marked by a commitment to ethical business practices and a deep respect for cultural traditions and environmental sustainability. A graduate of Texas Lutheran University (TLU) with a degree in International and Spanish Studies, and having spent time in Granada, Spain, and many other countries, Jimmy's global perspective has been enriched by extensive international experiences, further shaping his approach to business and leadership.

Jimmy's entrepreneurial spirit and innovative mindset have led him to spearhead groundbreaking projects, including a notable initiative in Guatemala. He became the first Ladino individual ever to be properly vetted and granted official permission by Mayan spiritual leaders—custodians of the region's volcanic panorama—to use volcanic rock for crafting 'mala' necklaces, bracelets, and other accessories. This approval not only showcases his respect for Indigenous traditions, but also reflects his ability to merge modern business practices with ancient wisdom. His reverence for these traditions is captured in one of his favorite quotes: "I listen to the advice from a volcano to stay active, to keep my inner fires burning, to know it's okay to let off steam, to go with the flow, to be uplifting and to have a blast!"

Alongside his innovative projects, Jimmy's professional journey is characterized by a strong focus on sustainable practices and social responsibility. His work often involves complex negotiations and partnerships across various business climates, always aiming to create outcomes that benefit his companies and the communities and environments they touch.

As a dedicated community member and mentor, Jimmy has contributed decades to coaching TLU Men's Soccer, for the most part on a pro bono basis, viewing it as a way to give back to the university and program that shaped him. His involvement in sports photography and coaching plays up his belief in the power of sports to teach valuable life skills such as teamwork, discipline, and perseverance.

As an ardent dog lover, Jimmy's companions over the years—Diego, Mia, and Chico—have added joy and inspiration to his life. His love for animals is matched by his connection to Brazil. His Brazilian brothers, Fabricio and Flavio, have deepened his affinity for Brazilian customs, enriching his personal and professional perspective.

Jimmy's actions for promoting positive change is evident in both his professional achievements and personal passions of soccer and newfound love for yoga. Whether mentoring young entrepreneurs, engaging in community development projects, or advocating for environmental conservation, Jimmy demonstrates the essence of a Good Vibe Gangsta who uses his influence and resources to make a significant impact.

In this book, Jimmy's experiences and philosophies serve as a guiding light for readers aspiring to integrate substantial personal growth with impactful entrepreneurial pursuits. His story encourages others to lead with integrity, embrace creative solutions, and contribute positively to the global community.

About Joey

Joey embodies the Good Vibe Gangsta spirit, blending a multicultural background with unwavering commitment to global entrepreneurship and social impact. His role as 'Dad' to his beloved daughter, María Alejandra, holds the highest place in his heart, reflecting his deep commitment to the Flores Family alongside his professional pursuits. His approach to business and life is deeply influenced by his appreciation of global communities, languages, and cuisines, which he has experienced firsthand through his extensive travels in both developed and developing countries.

Joey's nickname 'Bati' originated during his college soccer days at Texas Lutheran University (TLU), given to him by his teammate, Sean O'Brien. The nickname was a nod to Joey's physical resemblance and playing style, which mirrored those of Gabriel Batistuta, the famed Argentine striker known for his powerful playing style and prolific goal-scoring ability. This connection to such a sports legend reflects Joey's impactful approach not only on the soccer field but also in the international business and philanthropic worlds.

After earning a degree in International Business from TLU and an International MBA from St. Mary's University, Joey has used his education to navigate the complexities of international markets. However, it is his ongoing engagement with global communities that has most intelligently shaped his professional endeavors. Driven by the critical question, "Can you afford to care?" Joey co-created the 'Afford To Care' enterprise model, which integrates societal benefits into the core of commercial activities, ensuring that every business transaction helps address global social issues.

This commitment to ethical business practices and social responsibility has earned Joey global recognition, including an accolade from the U.S. Secretary of State for Corporate Excellence and The Rockefeller Foundation. Such honors underscore his role as a leader who not only seeks business success but also champions the welfare of communities worldwide. His presentations at prestigious venues like the New York Times building features his status as a thought leader in blending business success with ethical practices as was the focal point in his '40 Under 40' recognition by the San Antonio Business Journal.

Joey's life is a rich variety of experiences, with each adventure further enriching his understanding and appreciation of the world. His passion for travel and cultural exploration is matched by his dedication to making a significant impact on the communities he engages with. A few of his favorite extracurricular experiences include running with the bulls in Pamplona, Spain; juggling a soccer ball in the Maracaná while saluting the Cristo Redentor of Rio de Janeiro; climbing Mount Fuji in Japan; being at peace at the Vatican in Rome; enjoying a refreshing maté tea along Puerto Madero in Buenos Aires; appreciating the local couscous in an open air market in Tangier, Morocco; elevating the Eifel Tower in Paris; relaxing to the sounds of music festivals in Viña del Mar, Chile; testing the rushing waters of Niagara Falls in Canada; and strolling along the Thames River in London.

In this book, Joey shares these rich experiences and insights, inspiring readers to lead with compassion, respect diversity, and integrate a caring ethos into every aspect of their lives. His story encourages individuals to not only achieve personal and professional success but to do so in a way that contributes positively to the global community, embodying the true spirit of a Good Vibe Gangsta.

The Flores Brothers

Together, Jimmy and Joey are a dynamic duo, each bringing their unique strengths to their shared mission of promoting personal growth, social impact, and leadership. Their work and insights have been recognized by the Department of State of the United States of America, The Wall Street Journal and The Rockefeller Foundation, amongst many other major publications, affirming their roles as influential voices in global entrepreneurship and social impact. Their collaborative efforts have resulted not only in the success of creating and growing the VOS brand and its social impact but also in setting a benchmark for how businesses can operate with integrity and community focus.

Their recognition with the ACE Awards by the U.S. Department of State highlights their influence as international leaders who practice what they preach—integrating American values of development, responsibility, and diversity into every aspect of their operations. This accolade, given for their exemplary practices, places them among the ranks of global leaders, including individuals from companies like Coca-Cola, Boeing, Citibank, Dole, Esso, and Fruit of the Loom.

As seasoned experts in creating meaningful change, their combined efforts have not only carved a path in the business world but also significantly contributed to social impact initiatives worldwide. For their efforts as co-founders of the VOS brand, Jimmy and Joey were recognized as 'Entrepreneurs of the Year' for Guatemala by the Association of Guatemalan Executives, acknowledging them as top international entrepreneurs both regionally and globally.

The Flores Brothers operate on the principle that significant change can come from even the smallest actions. This philosophy drives their initiatives, encouraging others to recognize that they too can make a difference. Jimmy and Joey firmly believe that improving lives is a matter of deliberate actions and positive changes, not random chance.

Raised with a respectful regard for all individuals, regardless of their position or status, Jimmy and Joey were taught to value the janitor as much as the CEO. They measure success not by material wealth or accolades but by demonstrations of kindness, integrity, humility, generosity, and loyalty. These values are deeply embedded in every aspect of their lives and work, influencing how they conduct business, engage with communities, and interact with others.

The Flores Brothers uphold the principle that nothing is more valuable than a united family that prioritizes time over money. They understand that life is finite and, recognizing that everyone has an expiration date, they choose to trade money for time not the other way around. This philosophy has not only strengthened their familial bonds but also guided their life choices and business decisions, ensuring they make the most of every moment and leave a legacy that values relationships and personal fulfillment over fleeting material success.

Believing that small changes can create significant impacts, Jimmy and Joey consistently engage in efforts to give back on both local and global scales. They are driven by the conviction that improving others' lives does not happen by chance but through deliberate and positive changes. Their initiatives range from building educational programs and supporting health, wellness, and sports projects to creating economic opportunities for marginalized communities.

Together, Jimmy and Joey embody the essence of Good Vibe Gangstas, using their influence to promote positivity, resilience, and community-focused action. They lead by example, showing that successful business practices can harmoniously coexist with profound social impact. Their narrative reminds us that we all have the capacity to be agents of change, and that the journey towards a better world is paved with the efforts of those who dare to care deeply. The Flores Brothers continue to be luminaries in demonstrating how the Good Vibe Gangsta philosophy can transform lives and communities, ensuring a legacy that rings with positivity and hope.

The legacy that The Flores Brothers strive to build is one of impact and purpose—inspiring current and future generations to embrace compassion, integrity, and the relentless pursuit of positive transformation in their lives and the wider world. Jimmy and Joey firmly believe that even the smallest changes can lead to the biggest differences They continue to inspire new generations of leaders and changemakers to look beyond the traditional metrics of success and evaluate their impact on the world through how they contribute to the greater good.

Through this book, Jimmy and Joey offer more than theories on personal growth, social impact, and leadership; they provide a model derived from their own lives, demonstrating how personal experiences and cultural insights can shape a progressive business philosophy. Their stories are not just inspiring; they are practical examples of how to navigate the complexities of modern entrepreneurship while staying true to one's values and making a tangible impact on the world. Through their stories, The Flores Brothers hope to motivate others to champion the Good Vibe Gangsta philosophy—living a life filled with purpose, guided by ethics, and enriched by genuine connections and sustained contributions to society.

ACKNOWLEDGMENTS

Upon contemplating the path that has brought us to this book, we are incredibly grateful for every person, every obstacle, and every instance that has molded this endeavor. This book is a tribute to the tremendous support and inspiration we have received from so many people, as well as a reflection of our experiences and beliefs.

To Our Readers,

First, we would like to express our sincere gratitude to all our readers. This book would not exist without your passion and dedication to personal development, social impact and leadership. What truly makes these pages come to life is your willingness to embark on this journey with us, to discover and apply the ideals of a Good Vibe Gangsta to your own lives. We appreciate your support in our movement and for allowing us to share our vision with you.

To Our Family,

The foundation of our existence is deserving of deep appreciation. To our parents, whose unfailing love and moral direction have sculpted the very essence of who we are, and who first taught us the value of giving back and the power of love. Joey's daughter, María Alejandra, you are a constant source of delight and inspiration, motivating us daily to set examples that nurture, guide, and inspire.

A special and heartfelt homage goes to our late father, Mario Alejandro, whose soul and memories continue to guide us daily. Our hearts and the pages of this book are etched with the strength, integrity, and teachings you taught us, Dad. You instilled in us the value of diligence, the significance of integrity, and the power of kindness. Your life served as an example of the power one person can have in the world, and everyone who met you is still motivated by your legacy. Every kind deed we perform, every obstacle we overcome, every accomplishment of our goals—you are ever-present. We are grateful that you were our greatest benefactor, mentor, and hero. We make it a daily goal to follow your lead, and we intend to impart your wisdom to your granddaughter and future generations.

To our beloved mother, Rossi, whose grace and resilience have been the cornerstone of our upbringing—your influence is woven through every aspect of our lives and this book. Your endless support and nurturing have not only shaped us into the men we are today but have also instilled a deep-seated commitment to give back to the community that defines the essence of the Good Vibe Gangsta.

Your ability to nurture our independence while ensuring we stayed rooted in our cultural history and family values, and to strike a balance between strength and compassion, has been nothing short of inspirational. You instilled in us the value of education, the significance of empathy, and the indisputable force of caring deeply for others. With warmth and wisdom, your hands have held not only ours but also the hands of many others who have entered our circle.

And in times of challenge, supremely following the loss of our father, your resilience and capacity to support us through our loss while pursuing our goals have only served to deepen our regard and admiration for you. Your life teachings have served as our beam of hope, and your love has kept us going.

This book seeks to follow in your footsteps, to share the kindness and compassion you exude, and to uplift others in the same way that you have uplifted us. We are grateful to you, Mom, for being our constant support system, confidante, mentor, and one of the greatest grandmothers in the world. Every day, as we work to impact others' lives in the same way that you have impacted ours, we hope to make you proud of us and live up to the example you have set.

Acknowledging Contributors to Real-Life Examples

We extend our sincere gratitude to the people whose life experiences and tales enriched the 'Real-Life Examples' segments in every chapter of the book. Their desire to share their experiences has given rise to priceless insights that vividly illustrate the ideas presented in this book. Every narrative calls attention to the transforming potential of emulating the Good Vibe Gangsta philosophy in unique and significant ways.

Not only have each of you contributed to a chapter for this book, but your experiences have inspired readers as well. You embody the principles we cherish and believe in, and your examples serve as guides for our readers, encouraging them to pursue their paths with courage and integrity. Your stories serve as more proof that it is feasible to lead a compassionate life, live rejoicingly, and make a significant difference in the world. We are incredibly appreciative of your contributions and feel privileged to include your stories in this book.

We are grateful for your bravery in sharing, your openness to imparting knowledge, and your unwavering dedication to improving the world. Your involvement in this endeavor has greatly strengthened the message of the book by adding a rich layer of authenticity and valuable insights.

To Our Educators and Mentors,

We owe our professors, coaches, and mentors along the journey a debt of appreciation. From formal schooling to life's unofficial lessons, from playing fields to classrooms, you have pushed us, encouraged us, and believed in us even when the cards were stacked against us. Your insight and commitment have been foundational to our growth.

To Our Friends and Adversaries,

We are grateful to our friends for their constant support and the innumerable ways in which they have improved our lives. You have encouraged us to pursue greatness, supported us, and celebrated with us. Thank you also to those who doubted us and our opponents. Your challenges have sharpened our viewpoints and sustained our commitment. The tribulations and skepticism we encountered were invaluable, forcing us to reaffirm our commitment and refine our approach.

To Our Critics and Challenges,

We also acknowledge our detractors and the different difficulties we have faced. Every challenge, every unfavorable statement or deed, has served as a springboard for greater comprehension and fortitude. These experiences have shown us that resistance is the seed of tenacity and that positivity can, in fact, be created from negativity.

A Message of Positivity

Every adversity and every failure has given us a glimmer of hope—a chance to grow, adapt, and overcome. Because of this, the book is more than just a story; it is a celebration of the journey, complete with highs and lows. It is crafted with the hope that it will motivate you to turn setbacks into chances for development and virtuous deeds.

Closing Words

Thank you to everyone who has touched our lives and contributed to this journey. We hope that this book serves as a reminder that every interaction, every challenge, and every person you encounter carries with it the potential to change the world for the better. We leave you with a manifesto; let us continue to spread good vibes, respect, and build a legacy of positivity together.

With the deepest of gratitude,

The Flores Brothers

MANIFESTO

UNLEASH YOUR POWER, CONNECT AND GROW,
TOOLS IN HAND, LET YOUR TRUE COLORS SHOW.

CULTIVATE JOY, WHERE POSITIVITY THRIVES,
INNOVATE AND SUSTAIN AS YOUR SOUL STRIVES.

KNOWLEDGE EMPOWERS, WITH EACH LESSON TAUGHT,
INTEGRITY LEADS, WITH HONESTY WROUGHT.

BUILD A COMMUNITY, STAND UNITED IN CHEER,
LEAVE A LEGACY THAT WILL LAST YEAR AFTER YEAR.

FOR A WORLD OF CHANGE, LET'S ALL BAND TOGETHER,
GOOD VIBE GANGSTA, IMPROVING FOREVER.

GOODVIBEGANGSTA.COM

www.ingramcontent.com/pod-product-compliance
Lightning Source LLC
Chambersburg PA
CBHW050856160426
43194CB00011B/2183